William Allingham

Songs, Ballads and Stories

Including many now first collected, the rest rev. and rearranged

William Allingham

Songs, Ballads and Stories
Including many now first collected, the rest rev. and rearranged

ISBN/EAN: 9783744748179

Printed in Europe, USA, Canada, Australia, Japan

Cover: Foto ©Thomas Meinert / pixelio.de

More available books at **www.hansebooks.com**

SONGS BALLADS
AND
STORIES

BY WILLIAM ALLINGHAM

(AUTHOR OF "LAURENCE BLOOMFIELD" &c.)

INCLUDING MANY NOW FIRST COLLECTED
THE REST REVISED AND
REARRANGED

"Celsa ahunde petas"

LONDON
GEORGE BELL AND SONS
YORK STREET COVENT GARDEN
1877

CHISWICK PRESS:—CHARLES WHITTINGHAM,
TOOKS COURT, CHANCERY LANE.

CONTENTS.

DAY AND NIGHT SONGS.

	PAGE
"These little Songs"	3
A Holiday	4
Footsteps	5
Evey	7
Venus of the Needle	9
Across the Sea	10
The Bright Little Girl	11
The Fields in May	13
A Dream	14
In a Spring Grove	16
"Oh! were my Love"	16
The Ruined Chapel	18
The Cupids	19
Æolian Harp: "What saith the River?"	20
After Sunset	21
The Lighthouse	22
Serenade	23
We Two	24
The Wayside Well	25
The Lover and Birds	27
Æolian Harp: "Is it all in vain?"	29
"O Unknown Belov'd One!"	30
In a Broken Tower	31
The Witch Bride	32
Spring is Come	33
To Beata	34
The Messenger	36

The Valley Stream .
Autumnal Sonnet .
Angela .
The Choice
To Eärinè
Æolian Harp: "What is it that is gone?"
Late Autumn .
Our Mountain
"The Boy from his Bedroom Window".
"On the Longest Day" .
On a Forenoon of Spring
In Weimar .
The Poor Little Maiden .
Wayside Flowers .
The Cold Wedding
Half-Waking .
Winter Verdure
"Let us not teach and preach so much".
Æolian Harp: "O pale green Sea"
The Little Dell
"Levavi Oculos"
The Lullaby
"Sweet Looks! I thought them Love!"
Morning Plunge
On the Sunny Shore
Twilight Voices
By the Morning Sea
Love's Gifts
An Autumn Evening
Nightwind
The Statuette .
To Philippina .
A Boy's Burial
Frost in the Holidays
Would I Knew !

CONTENTS.

	PAGE
Under the Grass	83
Awaking	85
The Pilot's Daughter	86
On the Twilight Pond	89
To Plutus	90
His Town	91
Death Deposed	92
Winter Cloud	94
Danger	94
Recovery	95
Hymn	95
Rising of Jupiter	96
Cross-Examination	99
The Queen of the Forest	100
"O Spirit of the Summertime"	102
Æolian Harp: "Hear you now"	102
A Gravestone	104
A Vernal Voluntary	104
Two Moods	107
Mea Culpa	109
To the Nightingales	111
"Bare Twigs"	112
The General Chorus	113
Grapes, Wine, and Vinegar	114
In the Dusk	115
To Theodora	116
The Happy Man	117
Evening Prayer	118

BALLADS AND SONGS, &c.

Invitation to a Painter	121
Lovely Mary Donnelly	131
The Milkmaid	134
Abbey Asaroe	136

CONTENTS.

	PAGE
The Lupracaun	138
The Winding Banks of Erne	141
The Girl's Lamentation	146
The Abbot of Inisfalen	149
Kate of Ballyshanny	153
Among the Heather	155
The Nobleman's Wedding	156
The Fairies	158
St. Margaret's Eve	160
Thistledown	162
Wishing	164
The Bird	165
Here and There	166
Robin Redbreast	168
Down on the Shore	169
The Dirty Old Man	171
Two Fairies in a Garden	173
The Ballad of Squire Curtis	179
The Wondrous Well	183
The Maids of Elfin-Mere	184
Old Master Grunsey and Goodman Dodd	186
King Henry's Hunt	191
Kostas	194
Emily	196
The Shooting Star	198
Lady Alice	199
The Touchstone	201
A Wife	203
The Old Sexton	204
The Faithless Knight	205
The Mowers	206
Windlass Song	208
Homeward Bound	209
The Sailor	210
The Pilot Boat	212

CONTENTS.

	PAGE
Nanny's Sailor Lad	214
Cape Ushant	215
Civitas Dei	217

STORIES.

The Music-Master	221
Prince Brightkin	260
Southwell Park	277
George Hildebrand; or, The Schoolfellows	295
Mervaunee	305
"I know not if it may be mine"	327
Notes	329
Index of First Lines	337

ERRATUM.

Page 71, *for* "Troops of joy," *read* "Troops of joys."

DAY AND NIGHT SONGS.

B

THESE little Songs,
   Found here and there,
Floating in air
By forest and lea,
Or hill-side heather,
In houses and throngs,
Or down by the sea,—
Have come together,
How, I can't tell:
But I know full well
No witty goose-wing
On an inkstand begot 'em;
Remember each place
And moment of grace,
In summer or spring,
Winter or autumn,
By sun, moon, stars,
Or a coal in the bars,
In market or church,
Graveyard or dance,
When they came without search,
Were found as by chance.
A word, a line,
You may say are mine;
But the best in the songs,
Whatever it be,
To you, and to me,
And to no one belongs.

DAY AND NIGHT SONGS.

A HOLIDAY.

OUT of the city, far away
    With Spring to-day !—
Where copses tufted with primrose
    Give me repose,
Wood-sorrel and wild violet
    Soothe my soul's fret,
The pure delicious vernal air
    Blows away care,
The birds' reiterated songs
    Heal fancied wrongs.

Down the rejoicing brook my grief
    Drifts like a leaf,
And on its gently murmuring flow
    Doth glide and go ;
The bud-besprinkled boughs and hedges,
    The sprouting sedges
Waving beside the water's brink,
    Come like cool drink
To fever'd lips, like fresh soft mead
    To kine that feed.

Much happier than the kine, I bed
    My dreaming head
In grass; I see far mountains blue,
    Like heaven in view,
Green world and sunny sky above
    Alive with love;
All, all, however came they there,
    Divinely fair.

Is this the better oracle,
    Or what streets tell?
O base confusion, falsehood, strife,
    Man puts in life!
Sink, thou Life-Measurer!—I can say
    "I've lived a day;"
And Memory holds it now in keeping,
    Awake or sleeping.

FOOTSTEPS.

SOUND of feet
    In the lonely street,
Coming to-night,—coming to me?
Perhaps (why not? the thing may be)
    My dear old friend
    From the world's end,
      At last.
    How we shall meet,
    And shout and greet,
And talk of twenty things at once,
Till the first gush and rush be past,

And smoother now the current runs ;
Plenty on either side to tell,
Sharing joy, and soothing pain
As friendship's voice can do so well :
      Hush ! hark !
      I hear, in the dark—
Only the footsteps of the rain.

    Stay ! stay !
    Coming this way
Through the dull night—perhaps to me—
  Coming, coming, coming fast,
(And why may not such things be ?)
    A messenger's feet
    In the lonely street,
With some good wonderful news to say
    At last.
    A word has been spoken,
    A bad spell broken,
    Men see aright,
    All faces are bright,
For the world to-morrow begins anew,
And there's twenty million of things to do ;
Away ! search, sift the country through,
And say at once to a certain few :
    " Come, for our gain,
We know you, and now we have work for you."
      Hush ! hark !
      I hear, in the dark—
Only the footsteps of the rain.

Close, close,
Outside the house,
Steps approaching!—are these for me?
Coming gently, coming fast,
(And O, if this can be!)—
Out of the strife
Of selfish life
My Love has fled of a sudden,—'tis She,
At last!
Here she stands,
Eyes and mouth and tender form
True and warm;
My dream of many a lonely year;
Stretches her hands—
No doubt or fear—
" See, my Love, 'tis all in vain
To keep true lovers parted,
If they be faithful-hearted!"
Hush! hark!
I hear, in the dark—
Only the footsteps of the rain.

EVEY.

BUD and leaflet, opening slowly,
    Woo'd with tears by winds of Spring,
Now, of June persuaded wholly,
    Perfumes, flow'rs, and shadows bring,

Evey, in the linden alley,
    All alone I met to-day,
Tripping to the sunny valley
    Spread across with new-mown **hay**.

Brown her soft curls, sunbeam-sainted,
    Golden, in **the wavering flush**;
Darker brown her eyes are, painted
    Eye and fringe with **one** soft brush.

Through the leaves **a careless comer**,
    Never nymph of fount or tree
Could have press'd the floor **of summer**
    With a lighter **foot** than she.

Can this broad hat, fasten'd under
    With a bright blue ribbon's **flow**,
Change my pet so much, I wonder,
    Of **a** month or two ago?

Half too changed to **speak** I thought her,
    Till the pictured silence **broke**,
Sweet and clear as dropping water,
    Into words she sung or spoke.

Few her words; **yet,** like **a sister**,
    Trustfully she **look'd and smiled**;
'Twas but in my soul **I kiss'd** her,
    As I used to kiss the child.

Shadows, which are not of sadness,
    Touch her eyes, and brow above.
As pale wild roses dream of redness,
    Dreams her innocent heart of love.

VENUS OF THE NEEDLE.

O MARYANNE, you pretty girl,
   Intent on silky labour,
Of sempstresses the pink and pearl,
   Excuse a peeping neighbour!

Those eyes, for ever drooping, give
   The long brown lashes rarely;
But violets in the shadows live,—
   For once unveil them fairly.

Hast thou not lent that flounce enough
   Of looks so long and earnest?
Lo, here's more "penetrable stuff,"
   To which thou never turnest.

Ye graceful fingers, deftly sped!
   How slender, and how nimble!
O might I wind their skeins of thread,
   Or but pick up their thimble!

How blest the youth whom love shall bring,
   And happy stars embolden,
To change the dome into a ring,
   The silver into golden!

Who'll steal some morning to her side
   To take her finger's measure,
While Maryanne pretends to chide,
   And blushes deep with pleasure.

Who'll watch her sew her wedding-gown,
    Well conscious that it *is* hers;
Who'll glean a tress, without **a frown,**
    With those so ready scissors?

Who'll taste those ripenings of the **south,**
    The fragrant and delicious—
Don't put the pins into your mouth,
    O Maryanne, my precious!

I almost wish **it** were **my trust**
    To teach how shocking that **is**;
I wish **I** had **not, as** I must,
    To quit this tempting lattice.

Sure aim **takes** Cupid, fluttering **foe,**
    Across a street **so** narrow;
A thread of silk to string his **bow,**
    A needle for his arrow!

ACROSS THE SEA.

I WALK'D in the lonesome evening,
    And who so sad as I,
When I saw the young men and maidens
    Merrily passing by.

  To thee, my Love, to thee—
   So fain would I come to thee !
While the ripples fold upon sands of gold
   And I look across the sea.

 I stretch out my hands ; who will clasp them ?
   I call,—thou repliest no word :
 O why should heart-longing be weaker
   Than the waving wings of a bird !
  To thee, my Love, to thee—
   So fain would I come to thee !
For the tide's at rest from east to west,
   And I look across the sea.

 There's joy in the hopeful morning,
   There's peace in the parting day,
 There's sorrow with every lover
   Whose true-love is far away.
  To thee, my Love, to thee—
   So fain would I come to thee !
And the water's bright in a still moonlight,
   As I look across the sea.

THE BRIGHT LITTLE GIRL.

(To an Irish Tune.)

HER blue eyes they beam and they twinkle,
 Her lips have made smiling more fair ;
On cheek and on brow there's no wrinkle,
 But thousands of curls in her hair.

She's little,—you don't wish her taller;
   Just half through the teens is her age;
And baby or lady to call her,
   Were something to puzzle a sage.

Her walk is far better than dancing;
   She speaks as another might sing;
And all by an innocent chancing,
   Like lambkins and birds in the spring.

Unskill'd in the airs of the city,
   She's perfect in natural grace;
She's gentle, and truthful, and witty,
   And ne'er spends a thought on her face.

Her face, with the fine glow that's in it,
   As fresh as an apple-tree bloom—
And O! when she comes, in a minute,
   Like sunbeams she brightens the room.

As taking in mind as in feature,
   How many will sigh for her sake!
—I wonder, the sweet little creature,
   What sort of a wife she would make.

THE FIELDS IN MAY.

WHAT can better please,
    When your mind is well at ease,
Than a walk among the green fields in May?
    To see the verdure new,
    And to hear the loud cuckoo,
While sunshine makes the whole world gay:

    When the butterfly so brightly
    On his journey dances lightly,
And the bee goes by with business-like hum,
    When the fragrant breeze and soft
    Stirs the shining clouds aloft,
And the children's hair, as laughingly they come:

    When the grass is full of flowers,
    And the hedge is full of bowers,
And the finch and the linnet piping clear,
    Where the branches throw their shadows
    On a footway through the meadows,
With a brook among the cresses winding near.

    Any pair of lovers walking
    On this footway in sweet talking,
Sweeter silence, often linger and delay,
    For the path, not very wide,
    Brings them closer, side by side,
Moving gently through the happy fields of May:

   Till they rest themselves awhile
   At the elm-o'ershaded stile,
When stars begin to tremble in the blue,
   Just to hear a nightingale,
   Near our village in the vale,
To his sweetheart singing carols fond and true :

   Evening wind, and brooklet's flow,
   Softly whisper as they go,
Every star throbs with tenderness above ;
   Tender lips are sure to meet,
   Heart to heart must warmly beat,
When the earth is full and heaven is full of love.

   Oh, I would the song I sing
   Might to me a sweetheart bring,
For companion through the green fields of May!
   She should nestle in my heart,
   And we never more should part,
While the summers and the winters roll'd away.

A DREAM.

I HEARD the dogs howl in the moonlight night;
 I went to the window to see the sight;
All the Dead that ever I knew
Going one by one and two by two.

On they pass'd, and on they pass'd;
Townsfellows all, from first to last;
Born in the moonlight of the lane,
Quench'd in the heavy shadow again.

Schoolmates, marching as when we play'd
At soldiers once—but now more staid;
Those were the strangest sight to me
Who were drown'd, I knew, in the awful sea.

Straight and handsome folk; bent and weak too;
Some that I loved, and gasp'd to speak to;
Some but a day in their churchyard bed;
Some that I had not known were dead.

A long, long crowd—where each seem'd lonely,
Yet of them all there was one, one only,
Raised a head or look'd my way:
She linger'd a moment,—she might not stay.

How long since I saw that fair pale face!
Ah! Mother dear! might I only place
My head on thy breast, a moment to rest,
While thy hand on my tearful cheek were prest!

On, on, a moving bridge they made
Across the moon-stream, from shade to shade,
Young and old, women and men;
Many long-forgot, but remember'd then.

And first there came a bitter laughter;
A sound of tears the moment after;
And then a music so lofty and gay,
That every morning, day by day,
I strive to recall it if I may.

IN A SPRING GROVE.

HERE the white-ray'd anemone is born,
　Wood-sorrel, and the varnish'd buttercup;
And primrose in its purfled green swathed up,
Pallid and sweet round every budding thorn,
Gray ash, and beech with rusty leaves outworn.
Here, too, the darting linnet has her nest
In the blue-lustred holly, never shorn,
Whose partner cheers her little brooding breast,
Piping from some near bough. O simple song!
O cistern deep of that harmonious rillet,
And these fair juicy stems that climb and throng
The vernal world, and unexhausted seas
Of flowing life, and soul that asks to fill it,
Each and all these,—and more, and more, than these!

OH! WERE MY LOVE.

OH! were my Love a country lass,
　That I might see her every day,
And sit with her on hedgerow grass
　Beneath a bough of may;

And find her cattle when astray,
   Or help to drive them to the field,
And linger on our homeward way,
   And woo her lips to yield
A twilight kiss before we parted,
Full of love, yet easy-hearted.

Oh! were my Love a cottage maid,
   To spin through many a winter night,
Where ingle-corner lends its shade
   From fir-wood blazing bright.
Beside her wheel what dear delight
   To watch the blushes go and come
With tender words, that took no fright
   Beneath the friendly hum;
Or rising smile, or tear-drop swelling,
At a fire-side legend's telling.

Oh! were my Love a peasant girl,
   That never saw the wicked town;
Was never dight with silk or pearl,
   But graced a homely gown.
How less than weak were fashion's frown
   To vex our unambitious lot;
How rich were love and peace to crown
   Our green secluded cot;
Where Age would come serene and shining,
Like an autumn day's declining!

THE RUINED CHAPEL.

BY the shore, a plot of ground
   Clips a ruin'd chapel round,
Buttress'd with a grassy mound;
   Where Day and Night and Day go by,
And bring no touch of human sound.

Washing of the lonely seas,
Shaking of the guardian trees,
Piping of the salted breeze;
   Day and Night and Day go by
To the endless tune of these.

Or when, as winds and waters keep
A hush more dead than any sleep,
Still morns to stiller evenings creep,
   And Day and Night and Day go by;
Here the silence is most deep.

The empty ruins, lapsed again
Into Nature's wide domain,
Sow themselves with seed and grain
   As Day and Night and Day go by;
And hoard June's sun and April's rain.

Here fresh funeral tears were shed;
Now the graves are also dead;
And suckers from the ash-tree spread,
   While Day and Night and Day go by;
And stars move calmly overhead.

THE CUPIDS.

IN a grove I saw one day
  A flight of Cupids all at play,
Flitting bird-like through the air,
Or alighting here and there,
Making every bough rejoice
With a most celestial voice,
Or amongst the blossoms found
Rolling on the swarded ground.
Some there were with wings of blue,
Other some, of rosy hue,
Here, one plumed with purest white,
There, as dyed in golden light;
Crimson some, and some I saw
Colour'd like a gay macaw.
Many were the Queen of Beauty's—
Many bound to other duties.

A band of fowlers next I spied,
Spreading nets on every side,
Watching long, by skill or hap
Fleeting Cupids to entrap.
But if one at length was ta'en,
After mickle time and pain,
Whether golden one or blue,
Piebald, or of rosy hue,

When they put him in their cage
He grew meagre as with age,
Plumage rumpled, colour coarse,
Voice unfrequent, sad, and hoarse;
And little pleasure had they in him
Who had spent the day to win him.

ÆOLIAN HARP.

WHAT saith the river to the rushes gray,
    Rushes sadly bending,
    River slowly wending?
Who can tell the whisper'd things they say?
    Youth, and prime, and life, and time,
    For ever, ever fled away!

Drop your wither'd garlands in the stream,
    Low autumnal branches,
    Round the skiff that launches
Wavering downward through the lands of dream.
    Ever, ever fled away!
    This the burden, this the theme.

What saith the river to the rushes gray,
    Rushes sadly bending,
    River slowly wending?
It is near the closing of the day.
    Near the night. Life and light
    For ever, ever fled away!

Draw him tideward down; but not in haste.
    Mouldering daylight lingers;
    Night with her cold fingers
Sprinkles moonbeams on the dim sea-waste.
    Ever, ever fled away!
    Vainly cherish'd! vainly chased!

What saith the river to the rushes gray,
    Rushes sadly bending,
    River slowly wending?
Where in darkest glooms his bed we lay,
    Up the cave moans the wave,
    For ever, ever, ever fled away!

AFTER SUNSET.

THE vast and solemn company of clouds
    Around the Sun's death, lit, incarnadined,
Cool into ashy wan; as Night enshrouds
The level pasture, creeping up behind
Through voiceless vales, o'er lawn and purpled hill
And hazèd mead, her mystery to fulfil.
Cows low from far-off farms; the loitering wind
Sighs in the hedge, you hear it if you will,—
Though all the wood, alive atop with wings
Lifting and sinking throngh the leafy nooks,
Seethes with the clamour of ten thousand rooks.
Now every sound at length is hush'd away.
These few are sacred moments. One more Day
Drops in the shadowy gulf of bygone things.

THE LIGHTHOUSE.

THE plunging storm flies fierce against the pane,
    And thrills our cottage with redoubled shocks;
The chimney mutters and the rafters strain;
    Without, the breakers roar along the rocks.

See, from our fire and taper-lighted room,
    How savage, pitiless, and uncontroll'd
The grim horizon shows its tossing gloom
    Of waves from unknown angry gulfs uproll'd;

Where, underneath that black portentous lid,
    A long pale space between the night and sea
Gleams awful; while in deepest darkness hid
    All other things in our despair agree.

But lo! what star amid the thickest dark
    A soft and unexpected dawn has made?
O welcome Lighthouse, thy unruffled spark,
    Piercing the turmoil and the deathly shade!

By such a glimpse o'er the distracted wave
    Full many a soul to-night is re-possest
Of courage and of order, strong to save;
    And like effect it works within my breast.

Three faithful men have set themselves to stand
    Against all storms that from the sky can blow,
Where peril must expect no aiding hand,
    And tedium no relief may hope to know.

Nor shout they, passing brothers to inform
  What weariness they feel, or what affright;
But tranquilly in solitude and storm
  Abide from month to month, and show their light.

SERENADE.

OH, hearing sleep, and sleeping hear,
  The while we dare to call thee dear,
So may thy dreams be good, although
The loving power thou canst not know.
As music parts the silence,—lo!
Through heaven the stars begin to peep,
To comfort us that darkling pine
Because those fairer lights of thine
Have set into the Sea of Sleep.
Yet closèd still thine eyelids keep;
And may our voices through the sphere
Of Dreamland all as softly rise
As through these shadowy rural dells,
Where bashful Echo somewhere dwells,
And touch thy spirit to as soft replies.
  May peace from gentle guardian skies,
  Till watches of the dark be worn,
  Surround thy bed, and joyous morn
  Makes all the chamber rosy bright!
  Good-night!—From far-off fields is borne
  The drowsy Echo's faint "Good-night,"—
    Good-night! Good-night!

WE TWO.

LET all your looks be grave and cold,
    Or smile upon me still;
And give your hand, or else withhold;
    Take leave howe'er you will.
No lingering trace within your face
    Of love's regard is seen:
We two no more shall be—
    Never!—what we've been.

It is not now a longing day
    Divides us, nor a year;
Your heart from mine has turn'd away,
    Nor henceforth sheds a tear.
The winter snow may come and go,
    And April shadows green:
We two no more shall be—
    Never!—what we've been.

Ah, never! Countless hours, that bring
    Full many a chance and change,
May choose a beggar-boy for king,
    Or cleave a mountain-range.
The salt-sea tide may yet be dried
    That rolls far lands between:
We two no more can be—
    Never!—what we've been.

THE WAYSIDE WELL.

GREET thee kindly, Wayside Well,
    In thy hedge of roses!
Whither drawn by soothing spell,
    Weary foot reposes.

With a welcome fresh and green
    Wave thy border grasses,
By the dusty traveller seen,
    Sighing as he passes.

Cup of no Circean bliss,
    Charity of summer,
Making happy with a kiss
    Every meanest comer!

Morning, too, and eventide,
    Without stint or measure,
Cottage households near and wide
    Share thy liquid treasure.

Fair the greeting face ascends,
    Like a naiad daughter,
When the peasant lassie bends
    To thy trembling water.

When a laddie brings her pail
    Down the twilight meadow,
Tender falls the whisper'd tale,
    Soft the double shadow!

Clear as childhood is thy look,
    Nature **seems to** pet thee!
Fierce July that drains the brook
    Hath no power to fret thee.

Shelter'd cool and free from smirch
    In thy cavelet shady,
O'er thee in a silver birch
    Stoops a forest lady.

To thy glass the Star of **Eve**
    Shyly dares to bend her;
Matron Moon **thy** depths receive,
    Globed **in** mellow splendour.

Bounteous Spring! for ever own
    Undisturb'd thy station;
Not to thirsty lips alone
    Serving mild donation.

Never come the newt or frog,
    Pebble thrown in malice,
Mud or wither'd leaves, to **clog**
    Or defile **thy** chalice.

Heaven be still within thy ken,
    Through the veil thou wearest,—
Glimpsing clearest, as with men,
    When the boughs are barest!

THE LOVER AND BIRDS.

WITHIN a budding grove,
    In April's ear sang every bird his best.
But not a song to pleasure my unrest,
Or touch the tears unwept of bitter love.
Some spake, methought, with pity, some as if in jest.
        To every word
        Of every word
I listen'd, and replied as it behove.

    Scream'd Chaffinch, "Sweet, sweet, sweet!
Pretty lovey, come and meet me here!"
"Chaffinch," quoth I, "be dumb awhile, in fear
Thy darling prove no better than a cheat;
And never come, or fly when wintry days appear."
        Yet from a twig
        With voice so big,
The little fowl his utterance did repeat.

    Then I, "the man forlorn
Hears Earth send up a foolish noise aloft."
"And what'll *he* do? what'll *he* do!" scoff'd
The Blackbird, standing in an ancient thorn,
Then spread his sooty wings and flitted to the croft,
        With cackling laugh:
        Whom I, being half
Enraged, call'd after, giving back his scorn.

Worse mock'd the Thrush, "Die! die!
O could he do it? could he do it? Nay!
Be quick! be quick! Here, here, here!" (went
    his lay)
"Take heed! take heed!" then, "Why? why?
    why? why? why?
See—ee now! see—ee now!" (he drawl'd) "Back!
    back! back! R-r-r-run away!"
        O Thrush, be still!
        Or, at thy will,
Seek some less sad interpreter than I!

"Air, air! blue air and white!
Whither I flee, whither, O whither, O whither I
    flee!"
(Thus the Lark hurried, mounting from the lea)
"Hills, countries, many waters glittering bright,
Whither I see, whither I see! deeper, deeper, deeper,
    whither I see, see, see!"
        Gay Lark, I said,
        The song that's bred
In happy nest may well to heaven make flight.

"There's something, something sad,
I half remember "—piped a broken strain.
Well sung, sweet Robin! Robin sung again,
"Spring's opening cheerily, cheerily! be we glad!"
Which moved, I wist not why, me melancholy mad,
        Till now, grown meek,
        With wetted cheek,
Most comforting and gentle thoughts I had.

ÆOLIAN HARP.

IS it all in vain?
   Strangely throbbing pain,
Trembling joy of memory!
Bygone things, how shadowy
     Within their graves they lie!

Shall I sit then by their graves,
Listening to the melancholy waves?
    I would fain.
But even these in vapours die:
    For nothing may remain.

One survivor in a boat
On the wide dim deep afloat,
When the sunken ship is gone,
Lit by late stars before the dawn.

The sea rolls vaguely, and the stars are dumb.
   The ship is sunk full many a year.
     Dream no more of loss or gain.
   A ship was never here.
A dawn will never, never come.
    —Is it all in vain?

O UNKNOWN Belov'd One! to the mellow season
    Branches in the lawn make drooping bow'rs;
Vase and plot burn scarlet, gold, and azure;
Honeysuckles wind the tall gray turret,
    And pale passion-flow'rs.
Come thou, come thou to my lonely thought,
    O Unknown Belov'd One.

Now, at evening twilight, dusky dew down-wavers,
    Soft stars crown the grove-encircled hill;
Breathe the new-mown meadows, broad and misty;
Through the heavy grass the rail is talking;
    All beside is still.
Trace with me the wandering avenue,
    Thou Unknown Belov'd One.

In the mystic realm, and in the time of visions,
    I thy lover have no need to woo;
There I hold thy hand in mine, thou dearest,
And thy soul in mine, and feel its throbbing,
    Tender, deep, and true:
Then my tears are love, and thine are love,
    Thou Unknown Belov'd One!

Is thy voice a wavelet on the listening darkness?
    Are thine eyes unfolding from their veil?
Wilt thou come before the signs of winter—
Days that shred the bough with trembling fingers,
    Nights that weep and wail?
Art thou Love indeed, or art thou Death,
    O Unknown Belov'd One?

IN A BROKEN TOWER.

THE tangling wealth by June amass'd
   Left rock and ruin vaguely seen;
Thick ivy-cables held them fast,
   Light boughs descended, floating green.

Slow turn'd the stair, a breathless height,
   And, far above, it set me free,
When all the golden fan of light
   Was closing down into the sea.

A window half-way up the wall
   It led to; and so high was that,
The tallest trees were not so tall
   That they could reach to where I sat.

Aloft within the moulder'd tower
   Dark ivy fringed its round of sky,
Where slowly, in the deepening hour,
   The first faint stars unveil'd on high.

The rustling of the foliage dim,
   The murmur of the cool gray tide,
With tears that trembled on the brim,
   An echo sad to these I sigh'd.

O Sea, thy ripple's mournful tune!—
   The cloud along the sunset sleeps;
The phantom of the golden moon
   Is kindled in thy quivering deeps,

Oh, mournfully!—and I to fill,
   Fix'd in a ruin-window strange,
Some countless period, watching still
   A moon, a sea, that never change!

The guided orb is mounting slow;
   The duteous wave is ebbing fast;
And now, as from the niche I go,
   A shadow joins the shadowy past.

Farewell! dim ruins; tower and life;
   Sadly enrich the distant view!
And welcome, scenes of toil and **strife**;
   To-morrow's sun arises new.

THE WITCH-BRIDE.

A FAIR witch crept to a young man's side,
  And he kiss'd her and took her for his **bride**.

But a Shape came in at the dead of night,
And fill'd the room with snowy light.

And he saw how in **his** arms there lay
A thing more frightful than mouth may say.

And he rose in haste, **and** follow'd the Shape
Till morning crown'd an eastern cape.

And he girded himself and follow'd **still**,
When sunset sainted the western hill.

But, mocking and thwarting, clung to his side,
Weary day!—the foul Witch-Bride.

SPRING IS COME.

YE coax the timid verdure
   Along the hills of Spring,
Blue skies and gentle breezes,
   And soft clouds wandering!
The choir of birds on budding spray,
   Loud larks in ether sing;
A fresher pulse, a wider day,
   Give joy to everything.

The gay translucent morning
   Lies glittering on the sea,
The noonday sprinkles shadows
   Athwart the daisied lea;
The round sun's sinking scarlet rim
   In vapour hideth he,
The darkling hours are cool and dim,
   As vernal night should be.

Our Earth has not grown aged,
   With all her countless years;
She works, and never wearies,
   Is glad, and nothing fears:
The glow of air, broad land and wave,
   In season re-appears;
And shall, when slumber in the grave
   These human smiles and tears.

Oh, rich in songs and colours,
   Thou joy-reviving Spring!
Some hopes are chill'd with winter
   Whose term thou canst not bring.
Some voices answer not thy call
   When sky and woodland ring,
Some faces come not back at all
   With primrose-blossoming.

The distant-flying swallow,
   The upward-yearning seed,
Find nature's promise faithful,
   Attain their humble meed.
Great Parent! thou hast also form'd
   These hearts which throb and bleed;
With love, truth, hope, their life hast warm'd,
   And what is best, decreed.

TO BEATA.

I KNOW, I see, that you are fair,
   And so do other lips declare;
I love your face, I love your form;
My eyes grow dim, my heart grows warm,
With tender joy and pure affection,
At sight of these, or recollection.

And yet I could not nicely trace
From memory now your form and face;

I never sought to scrutinize
Your loveliness with curious eyes;
When with you, 'tis enough that I
So richly feel that you are nigh.

For I adore with fondest love
The earthly shape in which you move,
Being yours—not merely loving you
(Though you can gain such homage too)
Because your looks do also make
The promise which so many break.

The promise there is more than kept;
And deep love-founts, I know, have slept
In some hearts, till the power of God
In beauty's light material rod
Took shape and work'd a miracle—
But my love is a natural well.

A natural well, a centre given
To springs of earth and showers of heaven;
Whose earth-transmitted tinge of clay
Subsides at once, or melts away,
And leaves its heavenly birthplace shown,
In trembling softness of its own.

THE MESSENGER.

A MESSENGER, that stood beside my bed,
In words of clear and cruel import said
(And yet methought the tone was less unkind)
" I bring thee pain of body and of mind."

" Each gift of each must pay a toll to me ;
Nor flight, nor force, nor suit can set thee free ;
Until my brother come, I say not when :
Affliction is my name, unloved of men."

I swoon'd, then, bursting up in talk deranged,
Shatter'd to tears ; while he stood by unchanged.
I held my peace, my heart with courage burn'd,
And to his cold touch one faint sigh return'd.

Undreamt-of wings he lifted : " For a while
I vanish. Never be afraid to smile
Lest I waylay thee : curse me not ; nay, love ;
That I may bring thee tidings from above."

And often since, by day or night, descends
The face obdurate ; now almost a friend's.
O ! quite to Faith ; but Frailty's lips not dare
The word. To both this angel taught a pray'r.

" Lord God, thy servant, wounded and bereft,
Feels thee upon his right hand and his left :
Hath joy in grief, and still by losing gains ;—
All this is gone, yet all myself remains !"

THE VALLEY STREAM.

STREAM flowing swiftly, what music is thine!
    The breezy rock-pass, and the storm-wooing pine,
        Have taught thee their murmurs,
        Their wild mountain murmurs;
Subdued in thy liquid response to a sound
Which aids the repose of this pastoral ground;
Where our valley yet mingles an awe with the love
It smiles to the sheltering bastions above:
        Thy cloud-haunted birthplace,
        O Stream, flowing swiftly!

Encircle our meadows with bounty and grace;
Then move on thy journey with tranquiller pace,
        To find the great waters,
        The great ocean-waters,
Blue, wonderful, boundless to vision or thought;—
Thence, thence, might thy musical tidings be brought!
One waft of the tones of the infinite sea!
Our gain is but songs of the mountain from thee:
        Thy primitive issue,
        Thou Stream of our valley!

And have we divined what is thunder'd and hiss'd,
Where the awful ledge glimmers through screens of
    gray mist,
        And raves forth its secrets,
        The heart of its secrets?

Or learn'd what is hid in thy whispering note,
Mysteriously gather'd from fountains remote,
Where the solitudes spread in the upper sunshine?
O Stream flowing swiftly, what music is thine?
      Far-wafted, prophetic?
    Thou Stream of our valley!

AUTUMNAL SONNET.

NOW Autumn's fire burns slowly along the woods,
    And day by day the dead leaves fall and melt,
  And night by night the monitory blast
    Wails in the key-hole, telling how it pass'd
O'er empty fields, or upland solitudes,
    Or grim wide wave; and now the power is felt
Of melancholy, tenderer in its moods
    Than any joy indulgent summer dealt.
Dear friends, together in the glimmering eve,
    Pensive and glad, with tones that recognize·
  The soft invisible dew in each one's eyes,
It may be, somewhat thus we shall have leave
    To walk with memory, when distant lies
Poor Earth, where we were wont to live and grieve.

ANGELA.

AFTER the long bitter days, and nights weigh'
    down with my sadness,
Faint I lay on the sofa with soften'd thoughts in a twiligh

Stilly she glided in, and tenderly came she beside me,
Putting her arm round my head that was weary with
    sorrowful aching;
Whispering low, in a voice trembling with love and
    with pity,
" Knowest thou not that I love thee ?—am I not one
    in thy sorrow ?
Maze not thy soul in dark windings, joy that our Father
    excels us,
Since with His power extends the High One's care and
    compassion.
Fear not the losing of love; love is the surest of all things,
Heaven the birth-place and home of everything holy
    and lovely.
Go thou fearlessly on, unswerving from shades in thy
    pathway;
Pits and crags they seem, thou wilt find them nothing
    but shadows.
Take thou care of the present, thy future will build
    itself for thee.
Life in the body is full of entanglements, harsh con-
    tradictions;
Keep but the soul-realities, all will unwind itself duly.
Think of me, pray for me, love me—I cease not to
    love thee, my dearest."

So it withdrew and died. The heart, too joyful, too
    tender,
Felt a new fear of its pain, and its want, and the
    desolate evening

Sunken, and dull, and cold. But quickly a kind over-
 flowing
Soothed my feverish eyelids: **my spirit grew calmer**
 and calmer:
Noting, at length, **how the gloom** acknowledged a
 subtle suffusion,
Veiling with earnest peace **the stars looking in through**
 the window,—
Where, at the time appointed from **numberless** millions
 of ages,
Slowly, **up** eastern night, like a pale smoke **mounted**
 the moon-dawn.

THE CHOICE.

NOW let me choose a native blossom,
 Ere I quit the sunny fields,
Fitted for my Lucy's bosom,
 Hill, or brake, or meadow yields.

Flag or Poppy I'll not gather,
 Briony or Pimpernel;
Scented Thyme or sprouting Heather,
 Though I like them both so well.

Purpling **Vetches,** crimson Clover,
 Pea-bloom winglets, pied and faint,
Bluebell, Windflower, pass them over;
 Sober Mallow, Orchis quaint;

Striped Convolvulus in hedges,
   Columbine, and Mountain-Pink;
Lilies, floating seen through sedges,
   Violets nestling by the brink;

Creamy Elder, blue Germander,
   Betony that seeks the shade;
Nor where Honeysuckles wander,
   May that luscious balm persuade.

Sad Forget-me-not's a token
   Full of partings and mishaps;
Leave the Foxglove spire unbroken,
   Lest the fairies want for caps.

Crimson Loose-strife, Crowfoot, Pansy,
   Golden Gorse, or golden Broom,
Eyebright cannot fix my fancy,
   Nor the Meadowsweet's perfume.

Azure, scarlet, pink, or pearly,
   Rustic friends in field or grove—
Each of you I prize full dearly;
   None of you is for my Love!

Wild-Rose! delicately flushing
   All the border of the dale,—
Art thou like a pale cheek blushing,
   Or a red cheek turning pale?

Is it sorrow? Is it gladness?
   Lover's hopes, or lover's fears?
Or a most delicious sadness,
   Mingled up of smiles and tears?

Come!—no silky leaflet shaken—
    To a breast as pure and fair;
Come! and thoughts more tender waken
    Than thy fragrant spirit there!

TO EÄRINÈ.

> "Eärinè,
> Who had her very being, and her name,
> With the first knots or buddings of the Spring."
>   BEN JONSON.

SAINT Valentine kindles the crocus,
    Saint Valentine wakens the birds;
I would that his power could evoke us
    In tender and musical words!

I mean, us unconfident lovers,
    Whose doubtful or stammering tongue
No help save in rhyming discovers;
    Since what can't be said may be sung.

So, Fairest and Sweetest, your pardon
    (If no better welcome) I pray!
There's spring-time in grove and in garden;
    Perchance it may breathe in my lay.

I think and I dream (did you know it?)
    Of somebody's eyes, her soft hair,
The neck bending whitely below it,
    The dress that she chances to wear.

Each tone of her voice I remember,
  Each turn of her head, of her arm;
Methinks, had she faults out of number,
  Being hers, they were certain to charm.

From her every distance I measure;
  Each mile of a journey, I say—
" I'm so much the nearer my treasure,"
  Or " so much the further away."

And love writes my almanac also;
  The good days and bad days occur,
The fasts and the festivals fall so,
  By seeing or not seeing her.

Who know her, they're happy, they only;
  Whatever she looks on turns bright;
Wherever she is not, is lonely,
  Wherever she is, is delight.

So friendly her face that I tremble,
  On friendship so sweet having ruth:
But why should I longer dissemble?
  Or will you not guess at the truth?

And that is—dear Maiden, I love you!
  You sweetest, and brightest and best!—
Good luck to the roof-tree above you,
  The floor where your footstep is press'd!

May some new deliciousness meet you
  On every new day of the Spring;
Each flower in its turn bloom to greet you,
  Lark, mavis, and nightingale sing!

May kind vernal powers in your bosom
    Their tenderest influence shed!
May I, when the rose is in blossom,
    Enweave you a crown, white and red!

ÆOLIAN HARP.

WHAT is it that is gone, we fancied ours?
    O what is lost that never may be told?—
We stray all afternoon, and we may grieve
Until the perfect closing of the night.
Listen to us, thou gray Autumnal Eve,
Whose part is silence. At thy verge the clouds
Are broken into melancholy gold;
The waifs of Autumn and the feeble flow'rs
Glimmer along our woodlands in wet light;
Because within thy deep thou hast the shrouds
Of joy and great adventure, waxing cold,
Which once, or so it seem'd, were full of might.
Some power it was, that lives not with us now,
A thought we had, but could not, could not hold.
O sweetly, swiftly pass'd!—air sings and murmurs;
Green leaves are gathering on the dewy bough:
O sadly, swiftly pass'd!—air sighs and mutters;
Red leaves are dropping on the rainy mould.
Then comes the snow, unfeatured, vast, and white.
O what is gone from us, we fancied ours?

LATE AUTUMN.

OCTOBER—and the skies are cool and gray,
   O'er stubbles emptied of their latest sheaf,
  Bare meadow, and the slowly falling leaf.
The dignity of woods in rich decay
   Accords full well with this majestic grief
That clothes our solemn purple hills to-day,
   Whose afternoon is hush'd, and wintry brief.
Only a robin sings from any spray.
   And night sends up her pale cold moon, and spills
   White mist around the hollows of the hills,
Phantoms of firth or lake ; the peasant sees
His cot and stackyard, with the homestead trees,
   In-islanded ; but no vain terror thrills
His perfect harvesting ; he sleeps at ease.

OUR MOUNTAIN.

ALL hail to our Mountain ! form well-known !
   His skirts of heath, and his scalp of stone ;
Guardian of streams in their fitful youth,
Let them leap in spate or linger in drouth,—[1]
Who sets o'er the clouds an Olympian seat,
Where thunder is roll'd beneath our feet,
   Where storm and lightning
   And sunshine bright'ning
Solemnly girdle our steep retreat !

---

[1] *i.e.*, drought : an Ulster word has slipt in.

A Day on the Hills!—true king am I,
In my solitude, public to earth and sky.
Men have not tainted this atmosphere,
Wing'd thoughts only can follow here,
Folly and falsehood and babble stay
In the ground-smoke somewhere, far away.
    Let them greet and cheat
    In the narrow street,—
Who cares what all the newspapers say!

Oh, the tyrant eagle's palace to share,
And the loneliest haunts of the shy brown hare,—
The fields like a map, the lakes a-shine,
Hamlets and towns, and the ocean line,—
Beechen valley and bilberry dell,
And glen where the Echoes and Fairies dwell,
    With heaps and bosses
    Of plume-ferns and mosses,
Scarlet rowan and slight blue-bell!

Plume-ferns grow by the Waterfall,
Wide in the shimmering spray and tall,
Where the ash-twigs tremble, one and all,
And cool air murmurs, and wild birds call,
And the glowing crag lifts a dizzy wall
To the blue, through green leaves' coronal,
    And foam-bells twinkle
    Where sunlights sprinkle
The deep dark pool of the waterfall.

By a great cliff's foot, on the heather-flower,
I sit with the Shepherd Boy an hour,
Simple of life as his nibbling sheep,
Dotted far down the verdant steep;
I climb the path which sometimes fails
A peasant bound to more distant vales,
    When Night, descending,
    The world is blending,
Or fog, or the rushing blast, assails.

My feast on a marble block is spread,
I dip my cup in a cold well-head.
The poet's page is strong and fine,
I read a new volume in one old line,
Leap up for joy, and kiss the book;
Then gaze far forth from my lofty nook,
    With fresh surprise,
    And yearning eyes
To drink the whole beauty in one deep look.

From these towers the first gray dawn is spied,
They watch the last glimmer of eventide,
Wear shadows at noon, or vapoury shrouds,
And meet in council with mighty clouds;
And at dusk the ascending stars appear
On their pinnacle crags, or the chill moon-sphere.
    Whitening only
    Summits lonely,
Circled with gulfs of blackest fear.

When ripe and dry is the heathery husk,
Some eve, like a judgment-flame through the dusk,
It burns the dim line of a huger dome
Than is clad in the paschal blaze of Rome,
And to valley, river, and larch-grove spires,
Signals with creeping scarlet fires,
    Keen o'erpowering
    Embers cowering
Low where the western flush retires.

But the stern dark days with mutter and **moan**
Gather, like foes round a hated throne;
Terror is peal'd in the trumpet gale,
Crash'd **on** the cymbals of the hail,
Vapours move in a turbulent host,
Caves hold secret daggers of frost;
    And silently white
    In some morning's light
Stands the alter'd Mountain—a wintry ghost.

Till pack'd in hollows the round clouds lie,
And wild geese flow changing down the sky
To the salt sea-fringe; then milder rains
Course like young blood through the wither'd veins
That sweeping March left wasted and **weak**;
And the gray old Presence, dim and bleak,
    With sudden rally,
    O'er mound and **valley,**
Laughs with green light to his topmost peak!

Thy soft blue greeting through distant air
Is home's first smile to the traveller,—
Mountain, from thee, home's last farewell.
In alien lands there are tales to tell
Of thy haunted lake, and elvish ring,
And carn of an old Milesian king,
    And the crumbling turrets
    Where miser spirits
Batlike in vaults of treasure cling.

Giant! of mystical, friendly brow,
Protector of childhood's landscape thou,
Long golden seasons with thee abide,
And the joy of song, and history's pride.
Of all earth's hills I love thee best,
Reckon from thee mine east and west;
    Fondly praying,
    Wherever straying,
To leave in thy shadow my bones at rest.

THE Boy from his bedroom-window
    Look'd over the little town,
And away to the bleak black upland
    Under a clouded moon.

The moon came forth from her cavern;
    He saw the sudden gleam
Of a tarn in the swarthy moorland;
    Or perhaps the whole was a dream.

For I never could find that water
   In all my walks and rides:
Far-off, in the Land of Memory,
   That midnight pool abides.

Many fine things **had I glimpse of**,
   And said, " I shall find them **one day.**"
Whether within or without me
   They were, I cannot **say.**

O**N the** Longest **Day,**
   Heav'n was gay,
Roses and sunshine along **the** way.
   I loiter'd and stood,
   In listless **mood,**
   With many a sigh,
   I knew not why:
Nothing pleasant; nothing good.

   On the Shortest Day,
   Heav'n was gray,
Coldness and mire along the way.
   How **or** where
   Had I cast off care?
   For light and strong,
   With a snatch of song,
I stept through the mud and **biting air.**

.

Moods, that drift,
Or creep and shift,
Or change, not a windy cloud more swift,
No fetter found
To hold you bound,—
Can I dare to go
To the depth below
Whence ye rise, overspreading air and ground?

There in the gulf
Of my deep deep self,
Stranger than land of dragon and elf,
Acts and schemes,
Hopes and dreams,
Loves and praises,
Follies, disgraces,
Swarm, and each moment therewith teems.

They rise like breath
Of coming death,—
Of flow'rs that the soul remembereth,—
The Present, whose place
Is a footsole-space,
Being then as nought.
But the Present hath wrought
All this; and our Will is king, by God's grace.

ON A FORENOON OF SPRING.

I'M glad I am alive, to see and feel
   The full deliciousness of this bright day,
That's like a heart with nothing to conceal;
The young leaves scarcely trembling; the blue-gray
Rimming the cloudless ether far away;
Brairds,[1] hedges, shadows; mountains that reveal
Soft sapphire; this great floor of polish'd steel
Spread out amidst the landmarks of the bay.
I stoop in sunshine to our circling net
From the black gunwale; tend these milky kine
Up their rough path; sit by yon cottage-door
Plying the diligent thread: take wings and soar—
O hark, how with the season's laureate
Joy culminates in song! If such a song were mine!

IN WEIMAR.
(October, 1859.)

IN little German Weimar,
   With soft green hills enfolded,
Where shady Ilm-brook wanders,
   A Great Man lived and wrote;
In life and art and nature
He conn'd their "open secret,"
Of men and hours and fortunes
   He reverently took note.

---

[1] "Braird" means, in the north of Ireland, the first growth of young green corn of any sort. *Brord* (Ang.-Sax.) is "the first blade of corn or grass."

Upon a verge of Europe,
Facing the silent sunsets,
And loud Atlantic billows,
   For me, too, rose his thought,—
      Turn'd to a shape of stars on high
      Within the spiritual sky
      Of many an upward-gazing eye.

And now, this new October,
Within a holy garden,
'Mid flowers and trees and crosses,
   When dusk begins to fall,—
Where linden leaves are paling,
And poplar leaves are gilded,
And crimson is the wild-vine
   That hangs across the wall,—
I see the little temple
Wherein, with dust of princes,
The body lies of Goethe,
   And may not move at all.
      He mark'd all changes of the year;
      He loved to live; he did not fear
      The never-broken silence here.

Slow foots the gray old Sexton,
The ducal town's Dead-watcher,
Attending day and night time
   A bell that never rings;
The corpse upon the pallet,
A thread to every finger,—

The slightest touch would sound it,
　　But silence broods and clings.
Beside the room of stillness,
While yet his couch is warmer,
This old man hath his biding,
　　Therefrom the key he brings.
　　　　For mighty mortals, in his day,
　　　　He hath unlock'd the House of Clay,--
　　　　For *them*, as we are wont to say.

By yellow-leafy midwalk
Slow foots that aged Sexton;
"*Ja wohl!* I have seen Goethe,
　　And spoken too with him."
The lamp with cord he lowers,
And I, by steps descending,
Behold through grated doorway
　　A chamber chill and dim,—
Gaze on a dark red coffer:
Full fourscore years were counted,
When that grand head lay useless,
　　And each heroic limb.
　　　　Schiller's dust is close beside,
　　　　And Carl August's not far,—denied
　　　　His chosen place by princely pride.

The day had gloom'd and drizzled,
But clear'd itself in parting,
The hills were soft and hazy,
　　Fine colours streak'd the west,

(Above that distant ocean)
And Weimar stood before me,
A dream of half my lifetime,
   A vision for the rest:
The House that fronts the fountain,
The Cottage at the woodside,—
Long since I surely knew them,
   But still, to see was best.
      Town and Park for eyes and feet:
      But all th' inhabitants I greet
      Are Ghosts, in every walk and street.

THE POOR LITTLE MAIDEN.

A GENTLE face and clear blue eyes
   The little maiden hath, who plies
Her needle at her cottage door,
Or, with a comrade girl or more,
At times upon the hedgerow-grass.
I love to find her as I pass,—
Humbly contented, simply gay,
And singing sweetly; many a day
I've carried far along my way
From that fair infant's look and voice
A strength that made my soul rejoice.

O sad! her father died last week;
Her mother knows not where to seek
Five children's food; the little maid
Is far too young for others' aid.

Willingly would she do her best
To slave at strangers' rude behest;
But she is young and weak.   Her thread,
From dawn till blinding rushlight sped,
Could never win her single bread.

And must the Poorhouse save alive
This Mother and her helpless five,
Where Guardians, no Angelic band,
With callous eye and pinching hand,
Receive the wretched of their kin,
Cursing the **law that** lets them in?
I see her growing pale and thin,
Poor Child; **(the** little needle-song
Is ended)—and perhaps ere **long**
Her coffin jolting in their **cart**
To where the paupers lie **apart.**

Just from that cottage-step one sees
A Mansion with its lawn and trees,
Where man and wife are wearing old
In a wilderness of gold,
Amidst all luxuries and graces,
But the light of children's faces.
Ah, had the little Maid forlorn
In that fine house been only born,
How she were tended, night and morn!
A long-tail'd pony then were hers,
And winter mantles edged with furs,
And servants at her least command,
And wealthy suitors for her hand.

WAYSIDE FLOWERS.

PLUCK not the wayside-flower,
　　It is the traveller's dower;
A thousand passers-by
Its beauties may espy,
May win a touch of blessing
From Nature's mild caressing.
The sad of heart perceives
A violet under leaves
Like some fresh-budding hope;
The primrose on the slope
Like spots of sunshine dwells,
And cheerful message tells
Of kind renewing power;
The nodding bluebell's dye
Is drawn from happy sky.
Then spare the wayside-flower!
It is the traveller's dower.

THE COLD WEDDING.

BUT few days gone
　　Her hand was won
By suitor finely skill'd to woo;
　　And now come we
　　In pomp to see
The Church's ceremonials due.

The Bride in white
　Is clad aright,
Within her carriage closely hid ;
　No blush to veil—
　For too, too pale
The cheek beneath each downcast lid.

　White favours rest
　On every breast ;
And **yet** methinks we seem not gay.
　The church is cold,
　The priest is old,—
But who will give the bride away ?

　Now delver, stand,
　With spade in hand,
All mutely to discharge thy trust :
　Priest's words sound forth ;
　They're—" Earth to earth,
" Ashes to ashes, dust to dust."

　The groom is Death ;
　He has no breath ;
(The wedding peals, how slow they swing !)
　With icy grip
　He soon will clip
Her finger with a wormy ring.

　A match most fair.
　This silent pair,
Now to each other given for ever,

Were lovers long,
　　　Were plighted strong
In oaths and bonds that could not sever.

　　　Ere she was born
　　　That vow was sworn;
And we must lose into the ground
　　　Her face we knew:
　　　As thither you
And I, and all, are swiftly bound.

　　This Law **of** Laws
　　　That still withdraws
Each mortal from all mortal ken—
　　　If 'twere not here;
　　Or we saw clear
Instead of dim as now; what then?
This were not Earth, and we not Men.

HALF-WAKING.

I THOUGHT it was the little bed
　　I slept in long ago;
A straight white curtain at the head,
　　And two smooth knobs below.

I thought I saw the nursery fire,
　　And in a chair well-known
My mother sat, and did not tire
　　With reading all alone.

If I should make the slightest sound
　　To show that I'm awake,
She'd rise, and lap the blankets round,
　　My pillow softly shake;

Kiss me, and turn my face to see
　　The shadows on the wall,
And then sing *Rousseau's Dream* to me,
　　Till fast asleep I fall.

But this is not my little bed;
　　That time is far away;
'Mong strangers cold I live instead,
　　From dreary day to day.

WINTER VERDURE.

I SAT at home, and thought there lived no green,
　Because the time is winter; but, to-day,
Entering a park a mile or two away,
Smooth laurels tower'd as if no cold had been;
The tangled ivy, holly sharp and sheen,
Hung over nested ferns, and craglets gray
Broider'd with moss; high firs, a drooping screen,
Guarded their turfy lawn in close array.
Soon shall the hopeful woodbine-garland swing,
And countless buds the misty branch impearl:
My little Portress, fair come Spring to you—
Life's and the year's—flower-cheek'd and sparkling girl
Or are you, child, the Spirit of the Spring,
Safe in these warmer groves the winter through?

LET us not teach and preach so much,
  But cherish, rather than profess;
Be careful how the thoughts we touch
  Of God, and Love, and Holiness,—

A charm, most spiritual, faint,
  And delicate, forsakes our breast,
Bird-like, when it perceives the taint
  Of prying breath upon its nest.

Using, enjoying, let us live;
  Set here to grow, what should we do
But take what soil and climate give?
  For thence must come our sap and hue:

Blooming as sweetly as we may,
  Nor beckon comers, nor debar;
Let them take balm or gall away,
  According as their natures are:

Look straight at all things from the soul,
  But boast not much to understand;
Make each new action sound and whole,
  Then leave it in its place unscann'd:

Be true, devoid of aim or care;
  Nor posture, nor antagonise.
Know well that clouds of this our air
  But seem to wrap the mighty skies:

Search starry mysteries overhead,
   Where wonders gleam; yet bear in mind
That Earth's our planet, firm to tread,
   Nor in the star-dance left behind:

For nothing is withheld, be sure,
   Our being needed to have shown;
The far was meant to be obscure,
   The near was placed so to be known.

Cast we no astrologic scheme
   To map the course we must pursue;
But use the lights whene'er they beam,
   And every trusty landmark too.

The Future let us not permit
   To choke us in its shadow's clasp;
It cannot touch us, nor we it;
   The present moment's in our grasp.

Soul sever'd from the Truth is Sin;
   The dark and dizzy gulf is Doubt;
Truth never moves,—unmoved therein,
   Our road is straight and firm throughout.

This Road for ever doth abide.
   The universe, if fate so call,
May sink away on either side;
   But This and GOD at once shall fall.

ÆOLIAN HARP.

O PALE green sea,
  With long pale purple clouds above—
What lies in me like weight of love?
What dies in me
With utter grief, because there comes no sign
Through the sun-raying West, or on the dim sea-line?

O salted air,
Blown round the rocky headlands chill—
What calls me there from cove and hill?
What falls me fair
From Thee, the first-born of the youthful night?
Or in the waves is coming through the dusk twilight?

O yellow Star,
Quivering upon the rippling tide—
Sendest so far to one that sigh'd?
Bendest thou, Star,
Above where shadows of the dead have rest
And constant silence, with a message from the blest?

THE LITTLE DELL.

DOLEFUL was the land,
  Dull on every side,
Neither soft nor grand,
  Barren, bleak, and wide;

Nothing look'd with love ;
  All was dingy brown ;
The very skies above
  Seem'd to sulk and frown.

Plodding sick and sad,
  Weary day on day ;
Searching, never glad,
  Many a miry way ;
Poor existence lagg'd
  In this barren place ;
While the seasons dragg'd
  Slowly o'er its face.

Spring, to sky and ground,
  Came before I guess'd :
Then one day I found
  A valley, like a nest !
Guarded with a spell
  Sure it must have been—
This little fairy dell
  Which I had never seen.

Open to the blue,
  Green banks hemm'd it round ;
A rillet wander'd through
  With a tinkling sound ;
Briars among the rocks
  A tangled arbour made ;
Primroses in flocks
  Grew beneath their shade.

Merry birds a few,
   Creatures wildly tame,
Perch'd and sung and flew;
   Timid fieldmice came;
Beetles in the moss
   Journey'd here and there;
Butterflies across
   Danced through sunlit air.

There I often redd,
   Sung alone, or dream'd;
Blossoms overhead,
   Where the west wind stream'd;
Small horizon-line,
   Smoothly lifted up,
Held this world of mine
   In a grassy cup.

The barren land to-day
   Hears my last adieu:
Not an hour I stay;
   Earth is wide and new.
Yet, farewell, farewell!
   May the sun and show'rs
Bless that Little Dell
   Of safe and tranquil hours!

"LEVAVI OCULOS."

IN trouble for my sin, I cried to God;
  To the Great God who dwelleth in the deeps.
The deeps return not any voice or sign.

But with my soul I know thee, O Great God;
The soul thou gavest knoweth thee, Great God;
And with my soul I sorrow for my sin.

Full sure I am there is no joy in sin,
Joy-scented Peace is trampled under foot,
Like a white growing blossom into mud.

Sin is establish'd subtly in the heart
As a disease; like a magician foul
Ruleth the better thoughts against their will.

Only the rays of God can cure the heart,
Purge it of evil: there's no other way
Except to turn with the whole heart to God.

In heavenly sunlight live no shades of fear;
The soul there, busy or at rest, hath peace;
And music floweth from the various world.

The Lord is great and good, and is our God.
There needeth not a word but only these;
Our God is good, our God is great. 'Tis well.

All things are ever God's; the shows of things
Are of men's fantasy, and warp'd with sin;
God, and the things of God, immutable.

O great good God, my pray'r is to neglect
The shows of fantasy, and turn myself
To thy unfenced, unmeasured warmth and light!

Then were all shows of things a part of truth:
Then were my soul, if busy or at rest,
Residing in the house of perfect peace!

THE LULLABY.

I SEE two children hush'd to death,
   In lap of One with silver wings,
Hearkening a lute, whose latest breath
   Low lingers on the trembling strings.

Her face is very pale and fair,
   Her hooded eyelids darkly shed
Celestial love, and all her hair
   Is like a crown around her head.

Each ripple sinking in its place,
   Along the lute's faint-ebbing strain,
Seems echo'd slowlier from her face,
   And echo'd back from theirs again.

Yes, now is silence. Do not weep.
    Her eyes are fix'd : observe them long ;
And spell, if thou canst pierce so deep,
    The purpose of a nobler song.

SONG.

SWEET looks !—I thought them love ;
    Alas ! how much mistaken !
A dream a dream will prove,
    When time is come to waken.
She was friendly, fair, and kind ;
I was weak of wit, I find.
Hope, adieu !—for now I see
Her look of love, and not for me.

I see within her eyes
    A tender blissful token ;
Hope drops down and dies,
    But no sad word is spoken.
Soon and silent let me go ;
She, that knew not, shall not know.
Joy, good-bye !—for now I see
Her look of love, and not for me.

The fault was mine alone,
    Who from her gracious sweetness,
Made fancies all my own
    Of heavenly love's completeness,—

This from me, poor fool, as far
As from the earthworm shines the star.
Dream, farewell!—for now I see
Her look of love, and not for me.

MORNING PLUNGE.

I SCATTER the dreams of my pillow,
   I spring to a sunshiny floor;
O New Day!—how sparkles the billow,
   How brilliant are sea, sky, and shore!

The cliff with its cheerful adorning
   Of matted sea-pink under foot,
A lark gives me "top o' the morning!"
   A sailing-boat nods a salute.

Fresh-born from the foam, with new graces,
   Comes many a winsome fair maid,
Peep children's damp hair and bright faces
   From straw hat's or sun-bonnet's shade.

Green crystal in exquisite tremble,
   My tide-brimming pool I behold;
What shrimps on the sand-patch assemble!
   —I vanish! embraced with pure cold;

A king of the morning-time's treasures,
   To revel in water and air,
Join salmon and gull in their pleasures;
   Then home to our sweet human fare.

There stand the blue cups on white table,
　　Rich nugget of gold from the hive,
And there's uncle George and Miss Mabel,
　　And Kitty, the best child alive!

Now two little arms **round** my neck **fast,**
　　A kiss from a laugh I must win,—
You don't deserve one bit of breakfast,
　　You unbaptized people within!

ON THE SUNNY SHORE.

CHECQUER'D with woven shadows as I lay
　　Among the grass, blinking the watery gleam,—
I saw an Echo-Spirit in his bay,
Most idly floating in the noontide beam.
Slow heaved his filmy skiff, and fell, with sway
Of ocean's giant pulsing, and the Dream,
Buoy'd like the young moon on a level stream
Of greenish vapour at decline of day,
Swam airily,—watching the distant flocks
Of sea-gulls, whilst a foot in careless sweep
Touch'd the clear-trembling cool with tiny shocks,
Faint-circling; till at last he dropt asleep,
Lull'd by the hush-song of the glittering deep
Lap-lapping drowsily the heated rocks.

TWILIGHT VOICES.

NOW, at the hour when ignorant mortals
    Drowse in the shade of their whirling sphere,
Heaven and Hell from invisible portals
    Breathing comfort and ghastly fear,
        Voices I hear;
I hear strange voices, flitting, calling,
    Wavering by on the dusky blast,—
" Come, let us go, for the night is falling,
    Come, let us go, for the day is past!"

Troops of joy are they, now departed?
    Wingèd hopes that no longer stay?
Guardian spirits grown weary-hearted?
    Powers that have linger'd their latest day?
        What do they say?
What do they sing?   I hear them calling,
    Whispering, gathering, flying fast,—
" Come, come, for the night is falling;
    Come, come, for the day is past!"

Sing they to me?—" Thy taper's wasted;
    Mortal, thy sands of life run low;
Thine hours like a flock of birds have hasted;
    Time is ending;—we go! we go!"
        Sing they so?

Mystical voices, floating, calling;
   Dim farewells—the last, the last?—
"Come, come away, the night is falling;
   Come, come away, the day is past!"

See, I **am** ready, Twilight Voices;
   Child of the spirit-world am I;
How should I fear you? my soul rejoices.
     O speak plainer! O draw nigh!
         Fain would I fly!
Tell me your message, Ye who are calling
   Out of the dimness vague and vast?—
Lift me, take me,—the night is falling;
   Quick, let us go,—the day is past!

BY THE MORNING SEA.

THE wind shakes up the sleepy **clouds**
   To kiss the ruddied Morn,
And from their awful misty shrouds
   The mountains are new-born:
The Sea lies fresh with open eyes;
   Night-fears and moaning dreams
Brooding like clouds on nether skies,
   Have sunk below, and beams
Dance on the floor like golden flies,
   Or strike with joyful gleams
Some white-wing'd ship, a wandering **star**
Of Ocean, piloting afar.

In brakes, in woods, in cottage-eaves,
    The early birds are rife,
Quick voices thrill the sprinkled leaves
    In ecstasy of life;
With silent gratitude of flow'rs
    The morning's breath is sweet,
And cool with dew, that freshly show'rs
    Round wild things' hasty feet.
But heavenly guests of tranquil hours
    To inner skies retreat,
From human thoughts of lower birth
That stir upon the waking earth.

Across a thousand leagues of land
    The mighty Sun looks free,
And in their fringe of rock and sand
    A thousand leagues of sea.
Lo! I, in this majestic room,
    As real as the Sun,
Inherit this day and its doom
    Eternally begun.
A world of men the rays illume,
    GOD'S men, and I am one.
But life that is not pure and bold
Doth tarnish every morning's gold.

LOVE'S GIFTS.

THIS dark-brown curl you send me, Dear,
   Shall save its freshness of to-day
In gentle shrine, when year on year
   Have turn'd its former fellows gray;
So shall your image in my breast
With never-fading beauty rest.

What love hath once on love bestow'd,
   Translated, in its dew of youth,
To some remote divine abode,
   Withdraws from risk of time's untruth.
Keeping, we lose ; but what we give
Like to a piece of Heav'n doth live.

AN AUTUMN EVENING.

NOW is Queen Autumn's progress through the l:
   Her busy, sunbrown subjects all astir,
Preparing loyally on every hand
   A golden triumph. Earth is glad of her.

The regal curtainings of clouds on high,
   And shifting splendours of the vaulted air,
Express a jubilation in the sky,
   That nobly in the festival doth share.

With arching garlands of unfinger'd green,
    And knots of fruit, a bower each highway shows;
Loud busy Joy is herald on the scene
    To Gratitude, Contentment, and Repose.

Lately, when this good time was at its best,
    One evening found me, with half-wearied pace,
Mounting a hill against the lighted West,
    A cool air softly flowing on my face.

The vast and gorgeous pomp of silent sky
    Embathed a harvest realm in double gold;
Sheaf-tented fields of bloodless victory;
    Stackyards and cottages in leafy fold,

Whence climb'd the blue smoke-pillars. Grassy hill
    And furrow'd land their graver colourings lent;
And some few rows of corn, ungarner'd still,
    Like aged men to earth, their cradle, bent.

While reapers, gleaners, and full carts of grain,
    With undisturbing motion and faint sound
Fed the rich calm o'er all the sumptuous plain:
    Mountains, imbued with violet, were its bound.

Among the sheaves and hedges of the slope,
    And harvest-people, I descended slowly,
Field after field, and reach'd a pleasant group
    On their own land, that were not strangers wholly.

Here stood the Farmer, sturdy man though gray,
   In sober parley with his second son,
Who had been reaping in the rank all day,
   And now put on his coat, for work was done.

Two girls, like half-blown roses twin, that breathed
   The joy of youth untroubled with a care,
Laugh'd to their five-year nephew, as he wreathed
   Red poppies through his younger sister's hair.

Their homestead bounds received me with the rest,—
   The cheerful mother waiting at the door
Had smiles for all, and welcome for the guest,
   And bustling sought the choicest of her store.

O gentle rustic roof, and dainty board!
   Kind eyes, frank voices, mirth and sense were there:
Love that went deep, and piety that soar'd;
   The children's kisses and the evening pray'r.

Earth's common pleasures, near the ground like grass,
   Are best of all; nor die although they fade:
Dear, simple household joys, that straightway pass
   The precinct of devotion, undismay'd.

Returning homeward, soften'd, raised, and still'd;
   Celestial peace, that rare, transcendent boon,
Fill'd all my soul, as heav'n and earth were fill'd
   With bright perfection of the Harvest Moon.

NIGHTWIND.

M OANING blast,
   The summer is past,
And time and life are speeding fast.

   Wintry wind,
   Oh, where to find
The hopes we have left so far behind!

   Mystery cold,
   To thee have they told
Secrets the years may yet unfold?

   Sorrow of night,
   Is love so light
As to come and go like a breeze's flight?

   Opiate balm,
   Is death so calm
As to faint in one's ear like a distant psalm?

THE STATUETTE.

I DREAM'D that I, being dead a hundred years,
   (In dream-world, death is free from waking fears)
Stood in a City, in the market-place,
And saw a snowy marble Statuette,

Little, but delicately carven, set
Within a corner-niche. The populace
Look'd at it now and then in passing-by,
And some with praise. "Who sculptured it?" said I,
And then my own name sounded in my ears;
And, gently waking, in my bed I lay,
With mind contented, in the newborn day.

TO PHILIPPINA.

LADY fair, lady fair,
    Seated with the scornful,
Though your beauty be so rare,
    I were but a born fool
Still to seek my pleasure there.

To love your features and your hue,
    All your glowing beauty,
All in short, that's good of you,
    Was and is my duty,
As to love all beauty too.

But now a fairer face I've got,
    A Picture's—and believe me,
I never look'd to you for what
    A picture cannot give me:
What you've more, improves you not.

Your queenly lips can speak, and prove
  The means of your uncrowning;
Your brow can change, your eyes can move,
  Which grants you power of frowning;
Hers have Heav'n's one thought, of Love.

So now I give good-bye, *ma belle*,
  And lose no great good by it;
You're fair, yet I can smile farewell,
  As you must shortly sigh it,
To your bright, light outer shell!

A BOY'S BURIAL.

ON a sunny Saturday evening
    They laid him in his grave,
When the sycamore had not a shaking leaf,
    And the harbour not a wave.
The sandhills lay in the yellow ray
Ripe with the sadness of parting May;
Sad were the mountains blue and lone
That keep the landscape as their own;
The rocky slope of the distant fell;
The river issuing from the dell;—
And when had ended the voice of pray'r
The Fall's deep bass was left on the air,
        Rolling down.

Young he was and hopeful,
    And ah, to die so soon!
His new grave lies deserted
    At the rising of the moon;
But when morn comes round, and the church bells sound,
The little children may sit on the mound,
And talk of him, and as they talk,
Puff from the dandelion stalk
Its feathery globe, that reckons best
Their light-wing'd hours;—while the town is at rest,
And the stone-chat clacking here and there,
And the glittering Fall makes a tune in the air,
    Rolling down.

FROST IN THE HOLIDAYS.

THE time of Frost is the time for me!
    When the gay blood spins through the heart
        with glee,
When the voice leaps out with a chiming sound,
And the footstep rings on the musical ground;
When the earth is white, and the air is bright,
And every breath a new delight!

While Yesterday sank, full soon, to rest,
What a glorious sky!—through the level west
Pink clouds in a delicate greenish haze,
Which deepen'd up into purple grays,
With stars aloft as the light decreas'd,
Till the great moon rose in the rich blue east.

And Morning !—each pane a garden of frost,
Of delicate flow'ring, as quickly lost;
For the stalks are fed by the moon's cold beams,
And the leaves are woven like woof of dreams
By Night's keen breath, and a glance of the Sun
Like dreams will scatter them every one.

Hurra ! the lake is a league of glass !
Buckle and strap on the stiff white grass.
Off we shoot, and poise and wheel,
And swiftly turn upon scoring heel;
And our flying sandals chirp and sing
Like a flock of swallows upon the wing.

Away from the crowd with the wind we drift,
No vessel's motion so smoothly swift;
Fainter and fainter the tumult grows,
And the gradual stillness and wide repose
Touch with a hue more soft and grave
The lapse of joy's declining wave.

Pure is the ice; a glance may sound
Deep through an awful, dim profound,
To the water dungeons where snake-weeds hide,
Over which, as self-upborne, we glide,
Like wizards on dark adventure bent,
The masters of every element.

Homeward ! How the shimmering snow
Kisses our hot cheeks as we go !
Wavering down the feeble wind,

Like myriad thoughts in a Poet's mind,
Till the earth, and trees, and icy lakes,
Are slowly clothed with the countless flakes.

But our Village street—the stir and noise!
Where long black slides run mad with boys,
And *the pie is kept hot*, in sequence due,
Aristocrat now the hobnail shoe,
And the quaint white bullets fly here and there,
With laugh and shout in the wintry air!

In the clasp of Home, by the ruddy fire,
Ranged in a ring to our heart's desire,—
Now, who will tell some wondrous tale,
Almost to turn the warm cheeks pale,
Set chin on hands, make grave eyes stare,
Draw slowly nearer each stool and chair?

The one low voice goes wandering on
In a mystic world, whither all are gone;
The shadows dance; little Caroline
Has stolen her fingers up into mine.
But the night outside is very chill,
And the Frost hums loud at the window-sill.

WOULD I KNEW!

PLAYS a child in a garden fair
    Where the demigods are walking;
Playing unsuspected there
As a bird within the air,

Listens to their wondrous talking:
"Would I knew—would I knew
What it is they say and do!"

Stands a youth at city-gate,
   Sees the knights go forth together,
Parleying superb, elate,
Pair by pair in princely state,
   Lance and shield and haughty feather:
"Would I knew—would I knew
What it is they say and do!"

Bends a man with trembling knees
   By a gulf of cloudy border;
Deaf, he hears no voice from these
Winged shades he dimly sees
   Passing by in solemn order:
"Would I knew—O would I knew
What it is they say and do!"

UNDER THE GRASS.

WHERE these green mounds o'erlook the mingling Erne
And salt Atlantic, clay that walk'd as Man
thousand years ago, some Vik-ing stern,
May rest, or nameless Chieftain of a Clan;

And when my dusty remnant shall return
   To the great passive World, and nothing can
With eye, or lip, or finger, any more,
O lay it there too, by the river shore.

The silver salmon shooting up the fall,
   Itself at once the arrow and the bow;
The shadow of the old quay's weedy wall
   Cast on the shining turbulence below;
The water-voice which ever seems to call
   Far off out of my childhood's long-ago;
The gentle washing of the harbour wave;
Be these the sights and sounds around my grave.

Soothed also with thy friendly beck, my town,
   And near the square gray tower within whose shad
Was many of my kin's last lying-down;
   Whilst, by the broad heavens changefully array'd,
Empurpling mountains its horizon crown;
   And westward 'tween low hummocks is display'd,
In lightsome hours, the level pale blue sea,
With sails upon it creeping silently:

Or, other time, beyond that tawny sand,
   An ocean glooming underneath the shroud
Drawn thick athwart it by tempestuous hand;
   When like a mighty fire the bar roars loud,
As though the whole sea came to whelm the land —
   The gull flies white against the stormy cloud
And in the weather-gleam the breakers mark
A ghastly line upon the waters dark.

A green unfading quilt above be spread,
   And freely round let all the breezes blow;
May children play beside the breathless bed,
   Holiday lasses by the cliff-edge go;
And manly games upon the sward be sped,
   And cheerful boats beneath the headland row;
And be the thought, if any rise, of me,
What happy soul might wish that thought to be.

AWAKING.

A GOLDEN pen I mean to take,
   A book of ivory white,
And in the mornings when I wake
   The fair dream-thoughts to write,
Which out of heav'n to love are giv'n,
   Like dews that fall at night.
For soon the delicate gifts decay
As stirs the miry, smoky day.

"Sleep is like death," and after sleep
   The world seems new begun,
Its quiet purpose clear and deep,
   Its long-sought meaning won;
White thoughts stand luminous and firm
   Like statues in the sun;
Refresh'd from supersensuous founts
The soul to blotless vision mounts.

"Sleep is like death." Is death like sleep?
  —A waftage through still time?
And when its dreams of dawn shall peep
  What strange or alter'd clime
Will they foreshow? No man may know;
  Though some few souls may climb
So high as faintly to surmise
The master-secret of the skies.

THE PILOT'S DAUGHTER.

O'ER western tides the fair Spring Day
  Sent back a smile as it withdrew,
And all the harbour, glittering gay,
    Return'd a blithe adieu;
Great clouds above the hills and sea
Kept brilliant watch, and air was free
For last lark first-born star to greet,—
When, for the crowning vernal sweet,
Among the slopes and crags I meet
    The Pilot's pretty Daughter.

Round her gentle, happy face,
  Dimpled soft, and freshly fair,
Danced with careless ocean grace
    Locks of auburn hair:
As lightly blew the veering wind,
They touch'd her cheeks, or waved behind,

Unbound, unbraided, and unloop'd;
Or when to tie her shoe she stoop'd
Below her chin the half-curls droop'd,
    And veil'd the Pilot's Daughter.

Rising, she toss'd them gaily back,
  With gesture infantine and brief,
To fall around as smooth a neck
    As any wild-rose leaf.
Her Sunday frock of lilac shade
(That choicest tint) was neatly made,
And not too long to hide from view
The stout but noway clumsy shoe,
And stocking's trimly-fitting blue,
    That graced the Pilot's Daughter.

With look, half timid and half droll,
  And then with slightly downcast eyes,
And something of a blush that stole,
    Or something from the skies
Deepening the warmth upon her cheek,—
She turn'd when I began to speak;
The firm young step a sculptor's choice;
How clear the cadence of her voice!
Health bade her virgin soul rejoice,—
    The Pilot's lovely Daughter!

Were it my lot (the sudden wish)—
  To hand a pilot's oar and sail,
Or haul the dripping moonlight mesh,
    Spangled with herring-scale;

By dying stars, how sweet 'twould be,
And dawn-blow freshening the sea,
With weary, cheery pull to shore,
To gain my cottage-home **once more**,
And clasp, before **I reach** the door,
    My love, the Pilot's Daughter!

This element **beside my feet**
   Allures, a tepid wine of gold;
One touch, one taste, dispels the cheat,
   'Tis salt and nipping cold:
A fisher's hut, the scene perforce
Of narrow thoughts and manners coarse,
Coarse as the **curtains** that beseem
With net-festoons the smoky **beam**,
Would never **lodge my favourite dream**,
   Though fair **my Pilot's** Daughter.

To the large riches **of the earth,**
   Endowing men in their despite,
The *Poor*, by privilege of birth,
   Stand in the closest right.
Yet not alone the palm grows dull
With clayey **delve** and watery **pull**:
And **this** for me,—or hourly pain.
But could I sink and call it gain?
Unless a pilot true, 'twere vain
   To wed a Pilot's Daughter.

Lift *her*, perhaps?—but ah! I said,
  Much wiser leave such thoughts alone.
So may thy beauty, simple maid,
    Be mine, yet all thy own.
Join'd in my free contented love
With companies of stars above,
Who from their throne of airy steep
Do kiss these ripples as they creep
Across the boundless darkening deep,—
Low voiceful wave! hush soon to sleep
    The Pilot's gentle Daughter!

ON THE TWILIGHT POND.

A SHADOWY fringe the fir-trees make,
    Where sunset light hath been;
The liquid thrills to one gold flake,
    And Hesperus is seen;
Our boat and we, not half awake,
    Go drifting down the pond,
While slowly calls the Rail, "Crake-crake,"
    From meadow-flats beyond.

This happy, circling, bounded view
    Embraces us with home;
To far worlds, kindling in the blue,
    Our upward thoughts may roam;

Whence, with the veil of scented dew
   That makes the earth so sweet,
A touch of astral brightness too,
   A peace—which is complete.

TO PLUTUS.

PLUTUS, God of Riches, at thy shrine
   Floated never incense-wreath of mine,
Word of supplication, song of praise;
I despised thee in my early days,
Thee and all thy worshippers. Behold,
Youthful joy and courage waxing cold,
I am punish'd by thy powerful hand,
Proving well its manifold command.

All earth-hidden treasures are thy dower,
On the earth great mastery and power;
Park and palace thy goodwill assigns,
Dainty victuals and flow'r-fragrant wines;
Horses, chariots, pleasure-ships that go
Where the world is sweetest, to and fro;
Various joy of music, pictures, books,
Soft perpetual service, smiling looks;
Almost all the Gods I find thy friends;
Wise is he who at thine altar bends!
Cupid, Hymen, are thy sworn allies,
Scarcely doth Apollo thee despise.
Nay, 'twould seem as if the Powers at large
Gave this earth completely to thy charge.

I am now too old to change my ways ;
Still do I refuse thee prayer or praise ;
Change I will not, I'm too old a week,
Nor thine all-desirèd favour seek.
To thy vengeance, Earth-God !—power thou hast,
Not my adoration, first or last.

HIS TOWN.

HIS Town is one of memory's haunts,—
   Shut in by fields of corn and flax,
Like housings gay on elephants
    Heaved on the huge hill-backs.

How pleasantly that image came !
   As down the zigzag road I press'd,
·Blithe, but unable yet to claim
    His roof from all the rest.

And I should see my Friend at home,
   Be in the little town at last
Those welcome letters dated from,
    Gladdening the two years past.

I recollect the summer-light,
   The bridge with poplars at its end,
The slow brook turning left and right,
    The greeting of my friend.

I found him; he was mine,—his books,
　　His home, his day, his favourite walk,
The joy of swift-conceiving looks,
　　The glow of living talk.

July, no doubt, comes brightly still
　　On blue-eyed flax and yellowing wheat;
But sorrow shadows vale and hill
　　Since one heart ceased to beat.

Is not the climate colder there,
　　Since that Youth died?—it must be so;
A dumb regret is in the air;
　　The brook repines to flow.

Wing'd thither, fancy only sees
　　An old church on its rising ground,
And underneath two sycamore trees
　　A little grassy mound.

DEATH DEPOSED.

DEATH stately came to a young man, and said
　　　"If thou wert dead,
What matter?" The young man replied,
　　　"See my young bride,
Whose life were all one blackness if I died.
My land requires me; and the world's self, too,
Methinks, would miss some things that I can do."

Then Death in scorn this only said,
   " Be dead."
And so he was. And soon another's hand
   Made rich his land.
The sun, too, of three summers had the might
To bleach the widow's hue, light and more light,
   Again to bridal white.
And nothing seem'd to miss beneath that sun
   His work undone.

But Death soon met another man, whose eye
   Was Nature's spy;
Who said, " Forbear thy too triumphant scorn.
   The weakest born
Of all the sons of men, is by his birth
Heir of the Might Eternal; and this Earth
Is subject to him in his place.
   Thou leav'st no trace.

" Thou,—the mock Tyrant that men fear and hate,
   Grim fleshless Fate,
Cold, dark, and wormy thing of loss and tears!
   Not in the sepulchres
Thou dwellest, but in my own crimson'd heart;
Where while it beats we call thee Life. Depart!
A name, a shadow, into any gulf,
Out of this world, which is not thine,
   But mine:
  Or stay!—because thou art
   Only Myself."

WINTER CLOUD.

O NAMELESS Fear, which I would fain contemn!
   The swarthy wood-marge, skeleton'd with snow
Driv'n by a sharp north-east on bough and stem;
The broad white moor, and sable stream below
Blurr'd with gray smoke-wreaths wandering to and fro;
That monstrous cloud pressing the night on them,
Cloud without shape or colour, drooping slow
Down all the sky, and chill sleet for its hem;—
Such face of earth and time have I not watch'd
In other years: why now my spirit sinks,
Like captive who should hear, in helpless links,
Some gate of horror stealthily unlatch'd,
Who shows me? but Calamity methinks
Is creeping nigh, her cruel plot being hatch'd.

DANGER.

I STROVE for wicked peace, but might not win;
   The bonds would bite afresh, one moment slack.
"Then burst them!" .... instantly I felt begin
Damnation. Falling through a chasm of black,
I swiftly sunk thousands of miles therein.
Soul grew incorporate with gross weight of sin,
Death clung about my feet: let none dare track
My journey. But a far Voice call'd me back.
I breathe this world's infatuating air,

And tremble as I walk.   Most men are bold—
Perchance through madness.   O that I could hold
One path, nor wander to the fen, nor dare
Between the precipice and wild beast's lair!
For penalties are stablish'd from of old.

RECOVERY.

FOR many a day, like one whose limbs are stiff,
   Whose head is heavy with some grievous ail,
I felt, from wicked thoughts, the whole world drag
As millstone round my neck, all my force fail,
Dry up, and ravel into dust and rag.
But lo, I slept, and waking glad as if
I had been hearing music in my sleep,
Went forth, and look'd upon thy watery deep,
O King Unseen!—By stretch of some great hand
My sad, confus'd and fearful soul was shriv'n;
I knew the tranquil mind restored to me
To enjoy the colour of that pure blue heav'n,
Violet cloud-shadows on the greenish sea,
And rippling white foam on the yellow sand.

HYMN.

O HOW dimly walks the wisest
   On his journey to the grave,
Till Thou, Lamp of Souls, arisest,
   Beaming over land and wave!

Blind and weak behold him wander,
   Full of doubt and full of dread;
Till the dark is rent asunder,
   And the gulf of light is spread.

Shadows were the gyves that bound him;
   Now his soul is light in light;
Heav'n within him, Heav'n around him,
   Pure, eternal, infinite.

RISING OF JUPITER.

SPLENDIDLY Jupiter's Planet rises over the river,
   Jupiter, fabulous god of vanish'd mortals and
      years;
Silence and dusk diffused far and wide on the landscape,
   Solemn, shadowy world, past and present in one.
Many a glimmering light is aloft, but noblest to vision
   Now, as noblest in rank of our Sun's astonishing
      brood,
Over dim waters and woods and hills, in the clear dark
      night-sky,
   Jupiter hangs like a royal diamond, throbbing with
      flame.

Still in our starry heav'n the Pagan Gods have their
      station;
   Only, in sooth, as words: and what were they
      ever but words?
Lo, mankind hath fashion'd its thoughts, its hopes, and
      its dreamings,

Fashion'd and named them thus and thus, by the
voice of its bards,
Fashion'd them better or worse, from a shallower in-
sight or deeper,
Names to abide for a season, in many mouths or
in few;
Each and all in turn to give place, be it sooner or
later.
What is ten thousand years on the mighty Dial
of Heav'n?

Nothing is fix'd. All moves. O Star! thou hast
look'd upon changes
Here on this Planet of Man. Changes unguess'd
are to come.
The New Time forgetteth the Old,—remembereth
somewhat, a little,
A scheme, a fancy, a form, a word of the poet, a
name.
Still, when a deeper thought, a loftier, wider and truer,
Springs in the soul and flows into life, it cannot be
lost.
That which is gain'd for man is gain'd, as we trust, for
ever.
That which is gain'd is gain'd. We ascend, how-
ever it be.

Blaze, pure Jewel! Shine, O Witness, pulsing to mortals
Over the gulf of space a message in echoes of light.
Dead generations beheld thee, men unborn shall be-
hold thee,

H

Multitudes, wise and foolish, call thee by other
  words.
What was thy title of old, a beacon to wandering
    shepherds,
  Lifted in black-blue vault o'er the wide Chaldæan
    plain?
What is it now, Bright Star, at the wigwams out on
    the prairie?
  What between two pagodas at eve in the Flower
    Land?

Roll up the sky, vast Globe! whereuntó this other
    our dwelling,
  Is but the cat to the lion, the stalk of grass to the
    palm.
Certain to eye and thought,—but a very dream cannot
    reach thee,
  Glimpsing what larger lives may dwell in the
    spacious year.
Heed they at all, for their part, our little one-moon'd
    planet?
  Of China, India, or Hellas, or England, what do
    they know?
How have they named it, the spark our Earth, that we
    think so much of,
  One faint spark among many, with moon too small
    to be seen?

O great Space—great Spheres!—great Thought in the
    Mind!—what are ye?

O little lives of men upon earth!—O Planets
 and Moons!
Wheel'd and whirl'd in the sweep of your measured
 and marvellous motion,
Smoothly, resistlessly, swung round the strength of
 the central Orb,
Terrible furnace of fire — one lamp of the ancient
 abysses,
An Infinite Universe lighted with millions of
 burning suns,
Boundlessly fill'd with electrical palpitant world-form-
 ing ether,
Endlessly everywhere moving, concéntrating, well-
 ing-forth pow'r,
Life into countless shapes drawn upward, mystical spirit
 Born, that man—even we—may commune with
 God Most High.

CROSS-EXAMINATION.

WHAT knowest thou of this eternal code?
 As much as God intended to display.

Wilt thou affirm thou knowest aught of God?
 Nor save his works, that creature ever may.

Is not thy life at times a weary load?
 Which aimless on my back he would not lay.

Is it all good thy conscience doth forebode?
 The deepest thought doth least my soul affray.

When hath a glimpse of Heav'n been ever show'd?
   Whilst walking straight, I never miss its ray.

Why should such destiny to thee be owed?
   Easy alike to him are yea and nay.

Why shouldst thou reach it by so mean a road?
   Ask that of him who set us in the way.

Art thou more living than a finch or toad?
   Is soul sheer waste, if we be such as they?

Thou never wilt prevail to loose the node.
   If so, 'twere loss of labour to essay.

Nor to uproot these doubts so thickly sow'd.
   Nor thou these deeplier-rooted hopes to slay.

THE QUEEN OF THE FOREST.

BEAUTIFUL, beautiful Queen of the Forest,
   How art thou hidden so wondrous deep?
Bird never sung there, fay never morriced,
   All the trees are asleep.
   Nigh the drizzling waterfall
     Plumèd ferns wave and wither;
   Voices from the woodlands call,
     "Hither, O hither!"
   Calling all the summer day,
   Through the woodlands, far away.

Who by the rivulet loiters and lingers,
   Tranced by a mirror, a murmur, a freak;
Thrown where the grass's cool fine fingers
     Play with his dreamful cheek!

Cautious creatures gliding by,
    Mystic sounds fill his pleasure,
Tangled roof inlaid with sky,
    Flowers, heaps of treasure:
Wandering slowly all the day,
Through the woodlands, far away.

Late last night, betwixt moonlight and morning,
  Came She, unthought of, and stood by his bed;—
A kiss for love, and a kiss for warning,
    A kiss for trouble and dread.
Now her flitting fading gleam
    Haunts the woodlands wide and lonely;
Now, a half-remember'd dream
    For his comrade only,
He shall stray the livelong day
Through the forest, far away.

Dare not the hiding enchantress to follow!
  Hearken the yew, he hath secrets of hers.
The gray owl stirs in an oaktree's hollow,
    The wind in the gloomy firs.
Down among those dells of green,
    Glimpses, whispers, run to wile thee;
Waking eyes have nowhere seen
    Her that would beguile thee—
Draw thee on, till death of day,
Through the dusk woods, far away!

SONG.

O SPIRIT of the Summertime!
   Bring back the roses to the dells;
The swallow from her distant clime,
   The honey-bee from **drowsy** cells.

Bring back the friendship of the sun;
   The gilded evenings, calm and late,
When merry children homeward run,
   And peeping stars bid lovers wait.

Bring back the singing; and the scent
   Of meadowlands at dewy prime;—
Oh, **bring** again my heart's content,
   Thou **Spirit** of the Summertime!

ÆOLIAN HARP.

HEAR you now a **throbbing** wind that calls
   Over ridge **of cloud** and purple flake?
Sad the sunset's ruin'd palace-walls,
Dim the line of mist along the lake,—
Even as the mist of Memory.
O the summer-nights that used **to be**!

An evening rises from the dead
Of long-ago (ah me, how **long**!)
Like a story, like a song,

Told, and sung, and pass'd away.
Love was there, that since hath fled,
Hope, whose locks are turn'd to gray,
Friendship, with a tongue of truth,
And a beating heart of youth,
Wingèd Joy, too, just alighted,
Ever-welcome, uninvited ;
Love and Friendship, Hope and Joy,
With arms about each-other twined,
Merrily watching a crescent moon,
Slung to its gold nail of a star,
Over the fading crimson bar,
Like a hunter's horn : the happy wind
Breathed to itself some twilight tune,
And bliss had no alloy.

Against the colours of the west
Trees were standing tall and black,
The voices of the day at rest,
Night rose around, a solemn flood,
With fleets of worlds : and our delightful mood
Rippled in music to the rock and wood ;
Music with echoes, never to come back.
The touch upon my hand is this alone—
A heavy tear-drop of my own.

Listen to the breeze : " O loitering Time !—
" Unresting Time !—O viewless rush of Time !"
Thus it calls and swells and falls,
From Sunset's wasted palace-walls,
And ghostly mists that climb.

A GRAVESTONE.

FAR from the churchyard dig his grave,
   On some green mound beside the wave;
To westward, sea and sky alone,
And sunsets. Put a massy stone,
With mortal name and date, a harp
And bunch of hawthorn, carven sharp;
Then leave it free to winds that blow,
And patient mosses creeping slow,
And wandering wings, and footstep rare
Of human creature pausing there.

A VERNAL VOLUNTARY.

COME again, delightful Spring,
   Hasten, if you love us;
Let your woodbine-garland swing,
   Vault the blue above us!

Nay, already she is here:
   Stealthy laughters quiver
Through the ground, the atmosphere,
   Wood, and bubbling river.

Sweet the herald westwind blows,
Green peeps out from melting snows;
Snowdrop-flow'r, and crocus, dawn
With daffodil around the lawn;

Their bushy rods the sallows gild;
The clamorous rooks begin to build,
Watch the farmer dig and sow
In his miry fields below,
Gravely follow in the furrows
Picking where his plough unburrows.
Pearl-white lambkins frisk and bleat
Or kneeling tug the kindly teat;
The roguish rat is creeping nigh
His darksome cavern; low and high,
Through sun-gleam or soft rainy gloom,
Like children coursing every room
Of a new house, the swallows glance,
Wafted over Spain and France
From the sultry solemn Nile's
Mysterious lakes of crocodiles,
And the desert-lion's roar,
To a greener gentler shore.
Native lark from stair to stair
Of brilliant cloud and azure air
Mounts to the morning's top, and sings
His merry hymns on trembling wings,
Tireless, till the cressets high
Twinkle down from cooler sky.
What beholds he on this earth?
A rising tide of love and mirth.
—And was it I who lately said,
" Mirth is fled, and Love is dead,"
For chill and darkness on the day,
As on my weak and weary spirit lay?

Welcome, every breeze and show'r;
    Sun that courts the blossom;
Every new delicious flow'r
    Heap'd for Maia's bosom!

Every bird!—no bird alone,
    Always two together;
Spring inspiring every tone,
    Flushing every feather.

Verdure's tufted on the briar
Like crockets of a minster-spire;
Free sprouts the youngling corn; a light
Is on the hills; dim nooks grow bright
In blossom; now with scent and sight
And song, the childhood of the year
Renews our own; we see and **hear,**
We drink the fragrance, as of yore,—
A gleam, a thrill, a breath, no more.
Away, dull musing! who are these
Under the fresh-leaved linden trees?
Three favourite Children of the Spring,
Who lightly run, **as** half **on** wing,
Dorothy, Alicia, **Mary;**
Over moorlands wide **and airy,**
Deep in dells **of early flow'rs,**
They have been abroad for hours,
Flow'rs themselves, and fairer yet
Than primrose, windflow'r, violet,
Or even June's wild-rose to come.
Frost never touch their opening bloom

The tender fearless life to check!
—Alicia's hat is on her neck,
With flying curls and glowing face
And ringing laugh, she wins the race;
Her eyes were made for sorrow's cure,
And doubts of Heav'n to reassure.
Veils of fresh and fragrant rain
Sinking over the green plain,
Founts of sunny beams that lie
Scatter'd through the vernal sky,
The million-fold expanding woods,
Are less delightful than these children's moods.

'Tis not life, to pine and cloy;
   Sickness utters treason;
Best they live, who best enjoy
   Every good in season.

Glad, with moisten'd eyes, I learn
   April's own caressing:
Children, every month in turn
   Bring you three a blessing!

TWO MOODS.

I.

SLOW drags this dreary season;
   The earth a lump of lead;
The vacant skies, blue skies or brown,
   Bereft of joy and hope.

I cannot find a reason
 To wish I were not dead,—
Unfasten'd and let glide, gone down
 A dumb and dusky slope.
I recognize the look of care
In every face; for now I share
What makes a forehead wrinkles wear,
 And sets a mouth to mope.

A sombre, languid yearning
 For silence and the dark:
Shall wish, or fear, or wisest word,
 Arouse me any more?
 What profits bookleaf-turning?
 Or prudent care and cark?
Or Folly's drama, seen and heard
 And acted as before?
No comfort for the dismal Day;
It cannot work, or think, or pray;
A feeble pauper, sad and gray,
 With no good thing in store.

II.

 What lifts me and lightens?
 Enriches and brightens
The day, the mere day, the most marvellous day?
 O pleasure divine!
 An invisible wine
Pours quick through my being; broad Heaven is ben
And the Earth full of wonders, and both of them min(

What first shall I do, shall I say?
See the bareheaded frolicsome babes as they run
Go skipping from right foot to left foot in fun,—
    'Tis the pleasure of living;
    Too long I've o'erlook'd it,
    In sulk and misgiving,
    And lunatic fret;
    But it wakes in me yet,
    Though the world has rebuked it:
O city and country! O landscape and sun!
    Air cloudy or breezy,
    And stars, every one!
    Gay voices of children!
    All duties grown easy,
    All truths unbewild'ring,
Since Life, Life immortal, is clearly begun!

MEA CULPA.

AT me one night the angry moon,
    Suspended to a rim of cloud,
Glared through the courses of the wind.
Suddenly then my spirit bow'd
And shrank into a fearful swoon
That made me deaf and blind.

We sinn'd—we sin—is that a dream?
We wake—there is no voice nor stir;
Sin and repent from day to day,

As though some reeking murderer
Should dip his hand in a running stream,
And lightly go his way.

Embrace me, fiends and wicked men,
For I am of your crew.   Draw back,
Pure women, children with clear eyes.
Let Scorn confess me on his rack,—
Stretch'd down by force, uplooking then
Into the solemn skies!

Singly we pass the gloomy gate;
Some robed in honour, full of peace,
Who of themselves are not aware,
Being fed with secret wickedness,
And comforted with lies: my fate
Moves fast; I shall come there.

With all so usual, hour by hour,
And feeble will so lightly twirl'd
By every little breeze of sense,—
Lay'st thou to heart this common world?
Lay'st thou to heart the Ruling Power,
Just, infinite, intense?

Thou wilt not frown, O God.   Yet we
Escape not thy transcendent law;
It reigns within us and without.
What earthly vision never saw
Man's naked soul may suddenly see,
Dreadful, past thought or doubt.

TO THE NIGHTINGALES.

YOU sweet fastidious Nightingales!
   The myrtle blooms in Irish vales,
By Avondhu[1] and rich Lough Lene,[2]
Through many a grove and bowerlet green,
Fair-mirror'd round the loitering skiff.
The purple peak, the tinted cliff,
The glen where mountain-torrents rave
And foliage blinds their leaping wave,
Broad emerald meadows fill'd with flow'rs,
Embosom'd ocean-bays are ours
With all their isles; and mystic tow'rs
Lonely and gray, deserted long,—
Less sad if they might hear that perfect song!

What scared ye? (ours, I think, of old)
The sombre Fowl hatch'd in the cold?
King Henry's Normans, mail'd and stern,
Smiters of galloglas and kern?
Or, most and worst, fraternal feud,
Which sad Iernè long hath rued?
Forsook ye, when the Geraldine,
Great chieftain of a glorious line,
Was hunted on his hills and slain,
And one to France and one to Spain,

---

[1] The River Blackwater, in Munster.
[2] The old name of Killarney.

The remnant of the race withdrew?
Was it from anarchy ye flew,
And fierce oppression's bigot crew,
Wild complaint, and menace hoarse,
Misled, misleading voices, loud and coarse?

Come back, O Birds,—or come at last!
For Ireland's furious days are past;
And, purged of enmity and wrong,
Her eye, her step, grow calm and strong.
Why should we miss that pure delight?
Brief is the journey, swift the flight;
And Hesper finds no fairer maids
In Spanish bow'rs or English glades,
No loves more true on any shore,
No lovers loving music more.
Melodious Erin, warm of heart,
Entreats you;—stay not then apart,
But bid the Merles and Throstles know
(And ere another May-time go)
Their place is in the second row.
Come to the west, dear Nightingales!
The Rose and Myrtle bloom in Irish vales.

BARE twigs in April enhance our pleasure;
  We know the good time is yet to come;
With leaves and flow'rs to fill Summer's measure,
  And countless songs ere the birds be dumb.

Bare twigs in Autumn are signs for sadness;
  We feel the good time is well-nigh past;
The glow subdued, and the voice of gladness,
  And frosty whispers in every blast.

For perfect garlands just now we waited;
  Already, garlands are turning sere;
And Time, old traveller, like one belated,
  Hurries on to fulfil the year.

Ah, Spring's defects, and October's losses!
  Fair hope, sad memory!—but grieve not thou;
In leafless dells, look, what emerald mosses;
  Nay, secret buds on the wintry bough.

THE GENERAL CHORUS.

WE all keep step to the marching chorus,
  Rising from millions of men around.
Millions have march'd to the same before us,
  Millions come on, with a sea-like sound.
    Life, Death; Life, Death;
    Such is the song of human breath.

What is this multitudinous chorus,
  Wild, monotonous, low, and loud?
Earth we tread on, heaven that's o'er us?
  I in the midst of the moving crowd?
    Life, Death; Life, Death;
    What is this burden of human breath?

I

On with the rest, your footsteps timing!
  Mystical music flows in the song,
(Blent with it?—Born from it?)—loftily chiming
  Tenderly soothing, it bears you along.
    Life, **Death**; *Life,* **Death**;
      Strange **is the** chant of human breath!

GRAPES, WINE, AND VINEGAR.

WEARY and wasted, nigh worn-out,
    You sigh and shake white hairs, and say,
  "Ah, you will find the truth one **day**
Of Life and **Nature, do not** doubt!"

Age rhymes **to** sage, and let us give
    The hoary head its honours due:
    Grant **Youth** its privileges too,
And **notions how** to think and live.

Which has **more** chance to see aright
    The many-colour'd **shows** of time,
    Fresh human **eyes** in healthy prime
Or custom-dull'd and fading sight?

Gone from the primrose and the rose
    Their diversely delicious breath,
    Since no fine wafting visiteth
An old, perhaps **a** snuffy, **nose!**

Youth has its truth : I'd rather trust,
  Of two extremes, the ardent boy,
  Excess of life and hope and joy,
Than this dejection and disgust.

Vinegar of Experience—" drink ! "
  Why so, and set our teeth on edge ?
  Nay, even grant what you allege,
We'll not anticipate, I think.

Who miss'd, or loses, earlier truth,
  Though old, we shall not count him sage :
  Rare the strong mellow'd Wine of Age
From sunshine-ripen'd Grapes of Youth.

SONG,

IN THE DUSK.

O WELCOME! friendly stars, one by one, two by
  two ;
And the voices of the waterfall toning in the air ;
Whilst the wavy landscape-outlines are blurr'd with
    falling dew ;
  As my rapture is with sadness, because I may not
    share,
    And double it by sharing it with *thee.*
    —Cloudy fire dies away on the sea.

Now the calm shadowy earth she lies musing like a
    saint ;
  She is wearing for a halo the pure circlet of the moon ;

From the mountain breathes the night-wind, steadily
though faint ;
As I am breathing softly, "Ah ! might some heav'nly
boon
Bestow thee, my belov'd one, to my side !"
—Like a full, happy heart flows the tide.

TO THEODORA.

FROM HER HOPELESS BUT WORSHIPPING LOVER.

" Like the old age."—*Twelfth Night.*

THO' every dear perfection
    Be counsel for despair,
Far better my rejection
    Than thou less good or fair.

My peace of heart is troubled,
    I must not call thee mine ;
But all my world's ennobled,
    And life made more divine.

This earth, where'er I wander,
    Is richer as thy home,
The day more bright, and grander
    The midnight starry dome.

Man's dim heroic glory
    Its lustre doth renew ;
All heights in song or story
    Of love and faith, are true.

And tho' kind Heav'n completer
  Did thee than others make,
I count all women sweeter
  For thy beloved sake.

If sad, as too unworthy,
  Yet, happy in my mood,
I bless the Maker for thee,
  Who art so fair and good.

THE HAPPY MAN.

NO longer any choice remains;
  All beauty now I view,
All bliss that womankind contains,
  Completely summ'd in you.

Your stature marks the proper height;
  Your hair the finest shade;
Complexion—Love himself aright
  Each varying tint hath laid.
              No longer &c.

Your voice—the very tone and pitch
  Whereto my heart replies!
Blue eyes, or black, or hazel,—which
  Are best? *Your*-colour'd eyes.
              No longer &c.

Your manners, gestures, being of you,
  Most easily excel.
Have you defects? I love them too,
  I love yourself so well.
            No longer &c.

To me, once careworn, veering, vext,
  Kind fate my Queen hath sent;
In full allegiance, unperplext,
  I live in sweet content.

No longer any choice remains;
  All beauty now I view,
All bliss that womankind contains,
  Completely summ'd in you.

EVENING PRAYER.

GOOD LORD, to thee I bow my head;
  Protect me helpless in my bed;
May no ill dream disturb the night,
Nor sinful thought my soul affright;
And sacred sleep enfold me round,
As with a guardian-angel's wings,
From every earthly sight and sound;
While tranquil influence, like the dew
Upon thine outer world of things,
Prepares a morning fresh and new.

BALLADS AND SONGS, ETC.

BALLADS AND SONGS, ETC.

INVITATION TO A PAINTER,

SENT FROM THE WEST OF IRELAND.

I.

FLEE from London, good my Walter! boundless jail of bricks and gas,
Weary purgatorial flagstones, dreary parks of burnt-up grass,
Exhibitions, evening parties, dust and swelter, glare and crush,
Mammon's costly idle pomp, Mammon's furious race and rush;
Leave your hot tumultuous city for the breakers' rival roar,
Quit your small suburban garden for the rude hills by the shore,
Leagues of smoke for morning vapour lifted off a mountain-range,
Silk and lace for barefoot beauty, and for " something new and strange "
All your towny wit and gossip. You shall both in field and fair,
Paddy's cunning and politeness with the Cockney ways compare,
Catch those lilts and old-world tunes the maidens at their needle sing,

Peep at dancers, from an outskirt of the blithe applausive ring,
See our petty Court of Justice, where the swearing's very strong,
See our little plain St. Peter's with its kneeling peasant throng;
Hear the brogue and Gaelic round you; sketch a hundred Irish scenes,
(Not mere whisky and shillelagh)—wedding banquets, funeral *keenes;*
Rove at pleasure, noon or midnight; change a word with all you meet;
Ten times safer than in England, far less trammell'd in your feet.
    Here, the only danger known
    Is walking where the land's your own.
    Landscape-lords are left alone.

II.

We are barren, I confess it; but our scope of view is fine;
Dignifying shapes of mountains wave on each horizon-line,
So withdrawn that never house-room utmost pomp of cloud may lack,
Dawn or sunset, moon or planet, or mysterious zodiac.
Hills beneath run all a-wrinkle, rocky, moory, pleasant green;
From its Lough the Flood descending, flashes like a sword between,

Through our crags and woods and meadows, to the
   mounded harbour-sand,
To the Bay, calm blue, or, sometimes, whose Titanic
   arms expand
Welcome to the mighty billow rolling in from New-
   foundland.
Oats, potatoes, cling in patches round the rocks and
   boulder-stones,
Like a motley ragged garment for the lean Earth's
   jutting bones;
Moors extend, and bogs and furzes, where you seldom
   meet a soul,
But the Besom-man or woman, who to earn a stingy
   dole
Stoops beneath a nodding burden of the scented
   heather-plant,
Or a jolly gaiter'd Sportsman, striding near the grouse's
   haunt,—
Slow the anchoritic heron, musing by his voiceless
   pond,
Startled, with the startled echo from the lonely cliff
   beyond,
Rising, flaps away. And now a summit shows us,
   wide and bare,
All the brown uneven country, lit with waters here
   and there;
Southward, mountains—northward, mountains—west-
   ward, golden mystery
Of coruscation, when the Daystar flings his largesse
   on the sea;

Peasant cots with humble haggarts; mansions with
    obsequious groves;
A Spire, a Steeple, rival standards, which the liberal
    distance loves
To set in union. There the dear but dirty little
    Town abides,
And you and I come home to dinner after all our
    walks and rides.
    You shall taste a cleanly pudding;
    But, bring shoes to stand a mudding.

III.

Let me take you by the *murvagh*, sprinkled with the
    Golden Weeds
Merry troops of Irish Fairies mount by moonlight for
    their steeds,—
Wherefore sacred and abundant over all the land are
    they.
Many cows are feeding through it; cooling, of a sultry
    day,
By the River's brink, that journeys under Fairy Hill
    and past
Gentle cadences of landscape sloping to the sea at last
Now the yellow sand is round us, drifted in fantastic
    shapes,
Heights and hollows, forts and bastions, pyramid
    and curving capes,

    "Murvagh," sea-plain, level place near the sea, salt marsh.
    "Golden Weeds," ragwort, called "boughaleen bwee" (little yellow boy), also "fairy-horse."

Breezy ridges thinly waving with the bent-weed's
    pallid green,
Delicate for eye that sips it, till a better feast is seen
Where the turf swells thick-embroider'd with the
    fragrant purple thyme,
Where, in plots of speckled orchis, poet larks begin
    their rhyme,
Honey'd galium wafts an invitation to the gypsy bees,
Rabbits' doorways wear for garlands azure tufts of
    wild heartsease,
Paths of sward around the hillocks, dipping into ferny
    dells,
Show you heaps of childhood's treasure—twisted,
    vary-tinted shells
Lapt in moss and blossoms, empty, and forgetful of
    the wave.
Ha! a creature scouring nimbly, hops at once into his
    cave;
Brother Coney sits regardant,—wink an eye, and
    where is he?
Towns and villages we pass through, but the people
    skip and flee.
Over sandy slope, a Mountain lifts afar his fine blue
    head;
There the savage twins of eagles, gaping, hissing to
    be fed,
Welcome back their wide-wing'd parent with a rabbit
    scarcely dead
Hung in those powerful yellow claws, and gorge the
    bloody flesh and fur

On ledge of rock, their cradle. Shepherd-boy! with
    limbs and voice bestir
To your watch of tender lambkins on a lonesome
    valley-side,
If you, careless in the sunshine, see a rapid shadow glide
Down the verdant undercliff. Afar that conquering
    eye can sweep
Mountain-glens, and *moy*, and warren, to the margin
    of the deep,
Worse than dog or ferret;—vanish from your gold
    green-mossy dells,
Nibbling natives of the burrow! seek your inmost
    winding cells
    When such cruelties appear;
    But a Painter do not fear,
    Nor a Poet, loitering near.

IV.

Painter, what is spread before you? 'Tis the great
    Atlantic sea!
Many-colour'd floor of ocean, where the lights and
    shadows flee;
Waves and wavelets running landward with a sparkle
    and a song,
Crystal green with foam enwoven, bursting, brightly
    spilt along;
Thousand living shapes of wonder in the clear pool
    of the rock;

"Moy," plain.

Lengths of strand, and seafowl armies rising like a puff of smoke ;
Drift and tangle on the limit where the wandering water fails ;
Level faintly-clear horizon, touch'd with clouds and phantom sails;—
O come hither! weeks together let us watch the big Atlantic,
Blue or purple, green or gurly, dark or shining, smooth or frantic.
Far across the tide, slow-heaving, rich autumnal daylight sets ;
See our crowd of busy row-boats, hear us noisy with our nets,
Where the glittering sprats in millions from the rising mesh are stript,
Till there scarce is room for rowing, every gunwale nearly dipt ;
Gulls around us, flying, dropping, thick in air as flakes of snow,
Snatching luckless little fishes in their silvery overflow.
Now one streak of western scarlet lingers upon ocean's edge,
Now through ripples of the splendour of the moon we swiftly wedge
Our loaded bows; the fisher-hamlet beacons with domestic light ;
On the shore the carts and horses wait to travel through the night

To a distant city market, while the boatmen sup and sleep
While the firmamental stillness arches o'er the dusky
    deep,
    Ever muttering chants **and** dirges
    Round **its rocks** and **sandy** verges.

v.

Ere we part **at** winter's portal, **I shall** row you of a
    night
On **a** swirling Stygian **river, to a** ghostly yellow light.
When the nights are **black and gusty,** then do eels in
    myriads glide
Through the pools **and down the rapids, hurrying** to
    the ocean-tide,
(But they **fear the frost or** moonshine, in their mud-bed
    coiling close)
And **the** wearmen, on **the platform of** that pigmy
    water-house
Built among the river-currents, with **a dam to** either
    bank,
Pull the purse-net's **heavy end to** swing across their
    wooden tank,
Ere they loose the cord about it, then a slimy wriggling
    heap
Falls with splashing, **where a** thousand fellow-prisoners
    heave **and creep.**
Chill winds roar above the wearmen, darkling rush the
    floods below;
There they watch and work their eel-nets, till the late
    dawn lets them **go.**

There we'll join their eely supper, bearing smoke the best we can,
(House's furniture a salt-box, truss of straw, and frying-pan),
Hearken Con's astounding stories, how a mythologic eel
Chased a man o'er miles of country, swallow'd two dogs at a meal,
To the hissing bubbling music of the pan and *pratie-pot.*
Denser grows the reek around us, each like Mussulman a-squat,
Each with victuals in his fingers, we devour them hot and hot; ·
 Smoky rays our lantern throwing,
 Ruddy peat-fire warmly glowing,
 Noisily the River flowing.

VI.

Time's at hand, though, first of all, to journey to our Holy Well,
Clear as when the old Saint bless'd it, rising in its rock-bound cell.
Two great Crosses, carved in bosses, curves, and fillets interlacing,
Spread their aged arms of stone, as if in sempiternal blessing;
Five much-wrinkled thorntrees bend, as though in everlasting pray'r.
Greenly shines the growing crop, along the shelter'd hill-side there;

But the tristful little Abbey, crumbling among weeds and grass,
Nevermore can suns or seasons bring a smile to as they pass;
By a window-gap or mullion creeps the fringe of ivy leaves,
Nettles crowd the sculptured doorway, where the wind goes through and grieves;
Sad the tender blue of harebells on its ledges low and high;
Merry singing of the goldfinch there sounds pensive as a sigh.
'Tis a day of summer: see you, how the pilgrims wend along;
Scarlet petticoat, blue mantle, gray frieze, mingling in the throng.
By the pathway sit the Beggars, each an ailment and a whine;
Lame and sickly figures pass them, tottering in that pilgrim line;
Children carried by their parents, very loth to let them die;
Lovely girls too, with their eyelids downcast on a rosary;
Shrunken men, and witch-like women; young men in their proudest prime;
Guilty foreheads, hot-blood faces, penance-vow'd for secret crime.
All by turn, in slow procession, pace the venerable bounds,

   refoot, barehead, seven times duly kneeling in th' accustom'd rounds;
   rice among the hoary ruins, once before the wasted shrine,
   ace at each great carven cross, and once to form the Mystic Sign,
   ipping reverential finger in the Well, on brow and breast.
   eanwhile worn and wan, the Sick under those rooted thorntrees rest,
   aiting sadly. Here are human figures of our land and day,
   1 a thousand-years-old background,—still in keeping, it and they!
   alter, make a vow nor break it; turn your pilgrim steps our way.
     Oh might you come, before there fell
     One hawthorn-flow'r in Columb's Well!

LOVELY MARY DONNELLY.

(To an Irish Tune.)

OH, lovely Mary Donnelly, it's you I love the best!
   If fifty girls were round you I'd hardly see the rest.
  what it may the time of day, the place be where it will,
  eet looks of Mary Donnelly, they bloom before me still.

Her eyes like mountain water that's flowing on a rock
How clear they are, how dark they are! and they give
    me many a shock.
Red rowans warm in sunshine and wetted with a show'r
Could ne'er express the charming lip that has me in
    its pow'r.

Her nose is straight and handsome, her eyebrows lifted
    up,
Her chin is very neat and pert, and smooth like a china
    cup,
Her hair's the brag of Ireland, so weighty and so fine
It's rolling down upon her neck, and gather'd in a twine

The dance o' last Whit-Monday night exceeded all
    before,
No pretty girl for miles about was missing from the
    floor;
But Mary kept the belt of love, and O but she was
    gay!
She danced a jig, she sung a song, that took my heart
    away.

When she stood up for dancing, her steps were so
    complete,
The music nearly kill'd itself to listen to her feet;
The fiddler moan'd his blindness, he heard her so much
    praised,
But bless'd his luck to not be deaf when once her voice
    she raised.

And evermore I'm whistling or lilting what you sung,
Your smile is always in my heart, your name beside
    my tongue;
But you've as many sweethearts as you'd count on both
    your hands,
And for myself there's not a thumb or little finger
    stands.

Tis you're the flower o' womankind in country or in
    town;
The higher I exalt you, the lower I'm cast down.
If some great lord should come this way, and see your
    beauty bright,
And you to be his lady, I'd own it was but right.

O might we live together in a lofty palace hall,
Where joyful music rises, and where scarlet curtains
    fall!
O might we live together in a cottage mean and small,
With sods of grass the only roof, and mud the only
    wall!

O lovely Mary Donnelly, your beauty's my distress.
It's far too beauteous to be mine, but I'll never wish it
    less.
The proudest place would fit your face, and I am poor
    and low;
But blessings be about you, dear, wherever you may go!

THE MILKMAID.

(To the tune of " It was an old Beggarman.")

O WHERE are you going so early? he said;
Good luck go with you, my pretty maid;
To tell you my mind I'm half afraid,
   But I wish I were your sweetheart.
      When the morning sun is shining low,
      And the cocks in every farmyard crow,
        I'll carry your pail,
        O'er hill and dale,
      And I'll go with you a-milking.

I'm going a-milking, sir, says she,
Through the dew, and across the lea;
You ne'er would even yourself to me,
   Or take me for your sweetheart.
      When the morning sun, &c.

Now give me your milking-stool awhile,
To carry it down to yonder stile;
I'm wishing every step a mile,
   And myself your only sweetheart.
      When the morning sun, &c.

O, here's the stile in-under the tree,
And there's the path in the grass for me,
And I thank you kindly, sir, says she,
   And wish you a better sweetheart.
      When the morning sun, &c.

Now give me your milking-pail, says he,
And while we're going across the lea,
Pray reckon your master's cows to me,
   Although I'm not your sweetheart.
      When the morning sun, &c.

Two of them red, and two of them white,
Two of them yellow and silky bright,
She told him her master's cows aright,
   Though he was not her sweetheart.
      When the morning sun, &c.

She sat and milk'd in the morning sun,
And when her milking was over and done,
She found him waiting, all as one
   As if he were her sweetheart.
      When the morning sun, &c.

He freely offer'd his heart and hand;
Now she has a farm at her command,
And cows of her own to graze the land;
   Success to all true sweethearts!
      When the morning sun is shining low,
        And the cocks in every farmyard crow,
          I'll carry your pail
          O'er hill and dale,
      And I'll go with you a-milking.

ABBEY ASAROE.

GRAY, gray is Abbey Asaroe, by Ballyshanny town,
It has neither door nor window, the walls are broken down;
The carven-stones lie scatter'd in briar and nettle-bed;
The only feet are those that come at burial of the dead.
A little rocky rivulet runs murmuring to the tide,
Singing a song of ancient days, in sorrow, not in pride;
The elder-tree and lightsome ash across the portal grow,
And heaven itself is now the roof of Abbey Asaroe.

It looks beyond the harbour-stream to Gulban mountain blue;
It hears the voice of Erna's fall,—Atlantic breakers too;
High ships go sailing past it; the sturdy clank of oars
Brings in the salmon-boat to haul a net upon the shores;
And this way to his home-creek, when the summer day is done,
Slow sculls the weary fisherman across the setting sun;
While green with corn is Sheegus Hill, his cottage white below;
But gray at every season is Abbey Asaroe.

There stood one day a poor old man above its broken bridge;
He heard no running rivulet, he saw no mountain-ridge;

He turn'd his back on Sheegus Hill, and view'd with misty sight
The abbey walls, the burial-ground with crosses ghostly white;
Under a weary weight of years he bow'd upon his staff,
Perusing in the present time the former's epitaph;
For, gray and wasted like the walls, a figure full of woe,
This man was of the blood of them who founded Asaroe.

From Derry to Bundrowas Tower, Tirconnell broad was theirs;
Spearmen and plunder, bards and wine, and holy abbot's prayers;
With chanting always in the house which they had builded high
To God and to Saint Bernard,—whereto they came to die.
At worst, no workhouse grave for him! the ruins of his race
Shall rest among the ruin'd stones of this their saintly place.
The fond old man was weeping; and tremulous and slow
Along the rough and crooked lane he crept from Asaroe.

THE LUPRACAUN, OR FAIRY SHOEMAKER.

(A Rhyme for the Children.)

LITTLE Cowboy, what have you heard,
  Up on the lonely rath's green mound?
Only the plaintive yellow bird
  Sighing in sultry fields around,
Chary, chary, chary, chee-ee!—
Only the grasshopper and the bee?—
  " Tip-tap, rip-rap,
    Tick-a-tack-too!
Scarlet leather, sewn together,
  This will make a shoe.
Left, right, pull it tight;
  Summer days are warm;
Underground in winter,
  Laughing at the storm!"
Lay your ear close to the hill.
Do you not catch the tiny clamour,
Busy click of an elfin hammer,
Voice of the Lupracaun singing shrill
  As he merrily plies his trade?
    He's a span
    And a quarter in height.

  "Rath," ancient earthen fort.
  "Yellow bird," the yellow-bunting, or *yorlin*.

Get him in sight, hold him tight,
   And you're a made
     Man!

You watch your cattle the summer day,
Sup on potatoes, sleep in the hay;
  How would you like to roll in your carriage,
  Look for a duchess's daughter in marriage?
Seize the Shoemaker—then you may!
   " Big boots a-hunting,
     Sandals in the hall,
   White for a wedding-feast,
     Pink for a ball.
   This way, that way,
     So we make a shoe;
   Getting rich every stitch,
     Tick-tack-too!"
Nine-and-ninety treasure-crocks
This keen miser-fairy hath,
Hid in mountains, woods, and rocks,
Ruin and round-tow'r, cave and rath,
  And where the cormorants build;
     From times of old
     Guarded by him;
     Each of them fill'd
     Full to the brim
       With gold!

I caught him at work one day, myself,
  In the castle-ditch where foxglove grows,—

A wrinkled, wizen'd, and bearded Elf,
  Spectacles stuck on his pointed nose,
  Silver buckles to his hose,
  Leather apron—shoe in his lap—
    " Rip-rap, tip-tap,
      Tack-tack-too !
    (A grig skipp'd upon my cap,
      Away the moth flew !)
    Buskins for a fairy prince,
      Brogues for his son,—
    Pay me well, pay me well,
      When the job is done !"
The rogue was mine, beyond a doubt.
I stared at him ; he stared at me ;
" Servant, Sir !" " Humph !" says he,
  And pull'd a snuff-box out.
He took a long pinch, look'd better pleased,
  The queer little Lupracaun ;
Offer'd the box with a whimsical grace,—
Pouf ! he flung the dust in my face,
    And, while I sneezed,
      Was gone !

THE WINDING BANKS OF ERNE:

OR, THE EMIGRANT'S ADIEU TO BALLYSHANNY.[1]

(*A Local Ballad.*)

ADIEU to Ballyshanny! where I was bred and born;
Go where I may, I'll think of you, as sure as night and morn,
The kindly spot, the friendly town, where every one is known,
And not a face in all the place but partly seems my own;
There's not a house or window, there's not a field or hill,
But, east or west, in foreign lands, I'll recollect them still.
I leave my warm heart with you, though my back I'm forced to turn—
So adieu to Ballyshanny, and the winding banks of Erne!

No more on pleasant evenings we'll saunter down the Mall,
When the trout is rising to the fly, the salmon to the fall.
The boat comes straining on her net, and heavily she creeps,
Cast off, cast off!—she feels the oars, and to her berth she sweeps;

---

[1] The vernacular, and more correct, form of the name. See Notes.

Now fore and aft keep hauling, and gathering up the clew,
Till a silver wave of salmon rolls in among the crew.
Then they may sit, with pipes a-lit, and many a joke and " yarn ";—
Adieu to Ballyshanny, and the winding banks of Erne!

The music of the waterfall, the mirror of the tide,
When all the green-hill'd harbour is full from side to side—
From Portnasun to Bulliebawns, and round the Abbey Bay,
From rocky Inis Saimer to Coolnargit sandhills gray;
While far upon the southern line, to guard it like a wall,
The Leitrim mountains clothed in blue gaze calmly over all,
And watch the ship sail up or down, the red flag at her stern ;—
Adieu to these, adieu to all the winding banks of Erne!

Farewell to you, Kildoney lads, and them that pull an oar,
A lug-sail set, or haul a net, from the Point to Mullaghmore ;
From Killybegs to bold Slieve-League, that ocean-mountain steep,
Six hundred yards in air aloft, six hundred in the deep;
From Dooran to the Fairy Bridge, and round by Tullen strand,

Level and long, and white with waves, where gull and
 curlew stand;
Head out to sea when on your lee the breakers you
 discern!—
Adieu to all the billowy coast, and winding banks of
 Erne!

Farewell Coolmore,—Bundoran! and your summer
 crowds that run
From inland homes to see with joy th' Atlantic-setting
 sun;
To breathe the buoyant salted air, and sport among the
 waves;
To gather shells on sandy beach, and tempt the gloomy
 caves;
To watch the flowing, ebbing tide, the boats, the crabs,
 the fish;
Young men and maids to meet and smile, and form
 a tender wish;
The sick and old in search of health, for all things
 have their turn—
And I must quit my native shore, and the winding
 banks of Erne!

Farewell to every white cascade from the Harbour
 to Belleek,
And every pool where fins may rest, and ivy-shaded
 creek;
The sloping fields, the lofty rocks, where ash and holly
 grow,

The one split yew-tree gazing on the curving flood
    below;
The Lough, that winds through islands under Turaw
    mountain green;
And Castle Caldwell's stretching woods, with tranquil
    bays between;
And Breesie Hill, and many a pond among the heath
    and fern,—
For I must say adieu—adieu to the winding banks of
    Erne!

The thrush will call through Camlin groves the live-
    long summer day;
The waters run by mossy cliff, and banks with wild
    flowers gay;
The girls will bring their work and sing beneath a
    twisted thorn,
Or stray with sweethearts down the path among the
    growing corn;
Along the river side they go, where I have often been,—
O, never shall I see again the days that I have seen!
A thousand chances are to one I never may return,—
Adieu to Ballyshanny, and the winding banks of Erne

Adieu to evening dances, when merry neighbours meet,
And the fiddle says to boys and girls, "Get up and
    shake your feet!"
To "shanachus" and wise old talk of Erin's days
    gone by—

"Shanachus," old stories,—histories, genealogies.

Who trench'd the rath on such a hill, and where the
    bones may lie
Of saint, or king, or warrior chief; with tales of fairy
    power,
And tender ditties sweetly sung to pass the twilight hour.
The mournful song of exile is now for me to learn—
Adieu, my dear companions on the winding banks of
    Erne!

Now measure from the Commons down to each end
    of the Purt,
Round the Abbey, Moy, and Knather,—I wish no one
    any hurt;
The Main Street, Back Street, College Lane, the Mall,
    and Portnasun,
If any foes of mine are there, I pardon every one.
I hope that man and womankind will do the same by
    me;
For my heart is sore and heavy at voyaging the sea.
My loving friends I'll bear in mind, and often fondly
    turn
To think of Ballyshanny, and the winding banks of Erne.

If ever I'm a money'd man, I mean, please God, to
    cast
My golden anchor in the place where youthful years
    were pass'd;
Though heads that now are black and brown must
    meanwhile gather gray,
New faces rise by every hearth, and old ones drop
    away—

L

Yet dearer still that Irish hill than all the world beside;
It's home, sweet home, where'er I roam, through lands and waters wide.
And if the Lord allows me, I surely will return
To my native Ballyshanny, and the winding banks of Erne.

THE GIRL'S LAMENTATION.

(To an old Irish Tune.)

WITH grief and mourning I sit to spin;
   My Love pass'd by, and he didn't come in;
He passes by me, both day and night,
And carries off my poor heart's delight.

There is a tavern in yonder town,
My Love goes there and he spends a crown,
He takes a strange girl upon his knee,
And never more gives a thought to me.

Says he, "We'll wed without loss of time,
And sure our love's but a little crime;"—
My apron-string now its wearing short,
And my Love he seeks other girls to court.

O with him I'd go if I had my will,
I'd follow him barefoot o'er rock and hill;
I'd never once speak of all my grief
If he'd give me a smile for my heart's relief.

In our wee garden the rose unfolds,
With bachelor's-buttons, and marigolds;
I'll tie no posies for dance or fair,
A willow-twig is for me to wear.

For a maid again I can never be,
Till the red rose blooms on the willow tree.
Of such a trouble I've heard them tell,
And now I know what it means full well.

As through the long lonesome night I lie,
I'd give the world if I might but cry;
But I mus'n't moan there or raise my voice,
And the tears run down without any noise.

And what, O what will my mother say?
She'll wish her daughter was in the clay.
My father will curse me to my face;
The neighbours will know of my black disgrace.

My sister's buried three years, come Lent;
But sure we made far too much lament.
Beside her grave they still say a prayer—
I wish to God 'twas myself was there!

The Candlemas crosses hang near my bed;[1]
To look on them puts me much in dread,
They mark the good time that's gone and past:
It's like this year's one will prove the last.

---

[1] Little crosses woven of straw. A new cross is added each year, and the old ones are left till they fall to pieces.

The oldest cross it's a dusty brown,
But the winter winds didn't shake it down;
The **newest** cross keeps the colour bright,—
When the straw was reaping my heart was light.

The reapers rose **with the blink of morn,**
And gaily stook'd up the yellow corn,
To call them home **to the** field I'd run,
Through **the blowing breeze and the** summer sun.

When the straw was weaving my heart was glad,
For neither sin nor **shame I had,**
In the barn where oat-chaff **was** flying round,
And the thumping flails made a pleasant sound.

Now summer or winter to me **it's one**;
But oh! for a day like the time that's **gone.**
I'd little care was **it storm or shine,**
If I had but peace in this heart **of mine.**

Oh! light and false is **a young man's kiss,**
And a foolish **girl gives her soul** for this.
Oh! light **and short is the** young man's blame,
And a helpless **girl has the** grief and shame.

To the river-bank once I thought to **go,**
And cast myself in the stream **below;**
I thought 'twould carry us far out **to sea,**
Where they'd never find my poor babe and me.

Sweet Lord, forgive me that wicked mind!
You know I used to be well-inclined.
Oh, take compassion upon my state,
Because my trouble is so very great!

My head turns round with the spinning-wheel,
And a heavy cloud on my eyes I feel.
But the worst of all is at my heart's core;
For my innocent days will come back no more.

THE ABBOT OF INISFALEN.
(A KILLARNEY LEGEND.)

I.

THE Abbot of Inisfalen
   Awoke ere dawn of day;
Under the dewy green leaves
   Went he forth to pray.

The lake around his island
   Lay smooth and dark and deep,
And wrapt in a misty stillness
   The mountains were all asleep.

Low kneel'd the Abbot Cormac,
   When the dawn was dim and gray;
The prayers of his holy office
   He faithfully 'gan say.

Low kneel'd the Abbot Cormac,
   When the dawn was waxing red;
And for his sins' forgiveness
   A solemn prayer he said:

Low kneel'd that holy Abbot,
  When the dawn was waxing clear;
And he pray'd with loving-kindness
  For his convent-brethren dear.

Low kneel'd that blessed Abbot,
  When the dawn **was** waxing bright;
He pray'd a great prayer for Ireland,
  He pray'd with **all** his might.

Low kneel'd **that good old** Father,
  While the sun began to dart;
He pray'd a prayer for **all** mankind,
  He pray'd **it from his heart.**

II.

The Abbot of Inisfalen
  Arose upon his feet;
He heard a small bird singing,
  And O but it sung **sweet**!

He heard a **white** bird singing well
  Within a holly-tree;
A song so sweet and happy
  Never before heard **he.**

It sung upon a hazel,
  It sung upon **a** thorn;
He had never heard such music
  Since the hour **that he was born.**

It sung upon a sycamore,
    It sung upon a briar;
To follow the song and hearken
    This Abbot could never tire.

Till at last he well bethought him;
    He might no longer stay;
So he bless'd the little white singing-bird,
    And gladly went his way.

III.

But, when he came to his Abbey-walls,
    He found a wondrous change;
He saw no friendly faces there,
    For every face was strange.

The strange men spoke unto him;
    And he heard from all and each
The foreign tongue of the Sassenach,
    Not wholesome Irish speech.

Then the oldest monk came forward,
    In Irish tongue spake he:
"Thou wearest the holy Augustine's dress,
    And who hath given it to thee?"

"I wear the holy Augustine's dress,
    And Cormac is my name,
The Abbot of this good Abbey
    By grace of God I am.

"I went forth to pray, at the dawn of day;
  And when my prayers were said,
I hearken'd awhile to a little bird,
  That sung above my head."

The monks to him made answer,
  "Two hundred years have gone o'er,
Since our Abbot Cormac went through the gate,
  And never was heard of more.

"Matthias now is our Abbot,
  And twenty have pass'd away.
The stranger is lord of Ireland;
  We live in an evil day."

IV.

"Now give me absolution;
  For my time is come," said he.
And they gave him absolution,
  As speedily as might be.

Then, close outside the window,
  The sweetest song they heard
That ever yet since the world began
  Was utter'd by any bird.

The monks look'd out and saw the bird,
  Its feathers all white and clean;
And there in a moment, beside it,
  Another white bird was seen.

Those two they sang together,
    Waved their white wings, and fled;
Flew aloft, and vanish'd;
    But the good old man was dead.

They buried his blessed body
    Where lake and greensward meet;
A carven cross above his head,
    A holly-bush at his feet;

Where spreads the beautiful water
    To gay or cloudy skies,
And the purple peaks of Killarney
    From ancient woods arise.

KATE OF BALLYSHANNY.

(Air, "Moneymusk.")

SEEK up and down, both fair and brown,
    We've purty lasses many, O;
But brown or fair, one girl most rare,
    The Flow'r o' Ballyshanny, O.
As straight is she as poplar-tree,
    (Tho' not as aisy shaken, O,)
And walks so proud among the crowd,
    For queen she might be taken, O.
        From top to toe, where'er you go,
           The loveliest girl of any, O,—
           Ochone! your mind I find unkind,
              Sweet Kate o' Ballyshanny, O!

One summer day, the banks were gay,
    The Erne in sunshine glancin' there,
The big cascade its music play'd
    And set the salmon dancin' there.
Along the green **my Joy** was seen;
    Some goddess bright I thought her **there**;
The fishes, too, swam close, to view
    Her image in the water there.
        From **top to toe**, where'er **you go**,
          The loveliest girl of any, O,—
        Ochone! your mind I find unkind,
          Sweet Kate **o'** Ballyshanny, **O**!

My dear, give ear!—the river's near,
    And if you think I'm shammin' now,
To end my grief **I'll** seek relief
    Among the trout and salmon, **now**;
For shrimps and sharks to make their marks,
    And other watery vermin there;
Unless a mermaid saves my life,—
    My wife, and me her merman there.
        From top to toe, where'er you **go,**
          The loveliest girl of any, **O,**—
        Mavrone! your mind I find unkind,
          Sweet Kate o' Ballyshanny, **O**!

'Tis all in vain that I complain;
    No use to coax or chide her **there**;
As far away from me as Spain,
    Although I stand beside her there.

O cruel Kate ! since that's my fate,
   I'll look for love no more in you ;
The seagull's screech as soon would reach
   Your heart, as me implorin' you.
      Tho' fair you are, and rare you are,
         The loveliest flow'r of any, O,—
      Too proud and high,—goodbye, say I,
         To Kate o' Ballyshanny, O !

AMONG THE HEATHER.

(AN IRISH SONG.)

ONE evening walking out, I o'ertook a modest *colleen,*
   When the wind was blowing cool, and the harvest leaves were falling.
" Is our road, by chance, the same ? Might we travel on together ? "
" O, I keep the mountain side, (she replied) among the heather."

" Your mountain air is sweet when the days are long and sunny,
When the grass grows round the rocks, and the whin-bloom smells like honey ;
But the winter's coming fast, with its foggy, snowy weather,
And you'll find it bleak and chill on your hill, among the heather."

She praised her mountain home: and I'll praise it too, with reason,
For where Molly is, there's sunshine and flow'rs at every season.
Be the moorland black or white, does it signify a feather,
Now I know the way by heart, every part, among the heather?

The sun goes down in haste, and the night falls thick and stormy;
Yet I'd travel twenty miles to the welcome that's before me;
Singing hi for Eskydun, in the teeth of wind and weather!
Love'll warm me as I go through the snow, among the heather.

THE NOBLEMAN'S WEDDING.
(To an old Irish Tune.)

ONCE I was guest at a Nobleman's wedding;
  Fair was the Bride, but she scarce had been kind;
And now in our mirth, she had tears nigh the shedding;
  Her former true lover still runs in her mind.

Clothed like a minstrel, her former true lover
  Has taken his harp up, and tuned all the strings;
There among strangers, his grief to discover,
  A fair maiden's falsehood he bitterly sings.

" O here is the token of gold that was broken ;
   Through seven long years it was kept for your sake;
You gave it to me as a true lover's token ;
   No longer I'll wear it, asleep or awake."

She sat in her place by the head of the table,
   The words of his ditty she mark'd them right well ;
To sit any longer this bride was not able,
   So down, in a faint, from the carved chair she fell.

" O one, one request, my lord, one and no other,
   O this one request will you grant it to me?
To lie for this night in the arms of my mother,
   And ever, and ever, thereafter with thee."

Her one one request it was granted her fairly ;
   Pale were her cheeks as she went up to bed ;
And the very next morning, early, early,
   They rose and they found this young bride was dead.

The bridegroom ran quickly, he held her, he kiss'd her,
   He spoke loud and low, and listen'd full fain ;
He call'd on her waiting-maids round to assist her,
   But nothing could bring the lost breath back again.

O carry her softly ! the grave is made ready ;
   At head and at foot plant a laurel-bush green ;
For she was a young and a sweet noble lady,
   The fairest young bride that I ever have seen.

THE FAIRIES.

(A CHILD'S SONG.)

UP the airy mountain,
    Down the rushy glen,
We daren't go a hunting
    For fear of little men;
Wee folk, good folk,
    Trooping all together;
Green jacket, red cap,
    And white owl's feather!

Down along the rocky shore
    Some make their home,
They live on crispy pancakes
    Of yellow-tide foam;
Some in the reeds
    Of the black mountain-lake,
With frogs for their watch-dogs,
    All night awake.

High on the hill-top
    The old King sits;
He is now so old and gray
    He's nigh lost his wits.
With a bridge of white mist
    Columbkill he crosses,
On his stately journeys
    From Slieveleague to Rosses;

Or going up with music
   On cold starry nights,
To sup with the Queen
   Of the gay Northern Lights.

They stole little Bridget
   For seven years long;
When she came down again
   Her friends were all gone.
They took her lightly back,
   Between the night and morrow,
They thought that she was fast asleep,
   But she was dead with sorrow.
They have kept her ever since
   Deep within the lakes,
On a bed of flag-leaves,
   Watching till she wakes.

By the craggy hill-side,
   Through the mosses bare,
They have planted thorn-trees
   For pleasure here and there.
Is any man so daring
   As dig them up in spite,
He shall find their sharpest thorns
   In his bed at night.

Up the airy mountain,
   Down the rushy glen,
We daren't go a hunting
   For fear of little men;

Wee folk, good folk,
 Trooping all together;
Green jacket, red cap,
 And white owl's feather!

ST. MARGARET'S EVE.

I BUILT my castle upon the sea-side,
 The waves roll so gaily O,
Half on the land and half in the tide,
 Love me true!

Within was silk, without was stone,
 The waves roll so gaily O,
It lacks a queen, and that alone,
 Love me true!

The gray old harper sung to me,
 The waves roll so gaily O,
Beware of the Damsel of the Sea!
 Love me true!

Saint Margaret's Eve it did befal,
 The waves roll so gaily O,
The tide came creeping up the wall,
 Love me true!

I open'd my gate; who there should stand
 The waves roll so gaily O,
But a fair lady, with a cup in her hand,
 Love me true!

The cup was gold, and full of wine,
   The waves roll so gaily O,
Drink, said the lady, and I will be thine,
   Love me true!

Enter my castle, lady fair,
   The waves roll so gaily O,
You shall be queen of all that's there,
   Love me true!

A gray old harper sung to me,
   The waves roll so gaily O,
Beware of the Damsel of the Sea!
   Love me true!

In hall he harpeth many a year,
   The waves roll so gaily O,
And we will sit his song to hear,
   Love me true!

I love thee deep, I love thee true,
   The waves roll so gaily O,
But ah! I know not how to woo,
   Love me true!

Down dash'd the cup, with a sudden shock,
   The waves roll so gaily O,
The wine like blood ran over the rock,
   Love me true!

She said no word, but shriek'd aloud,
  The waves roll so gaily O,
And vanish'd away from where she stood,
  Love me true!

I lock'd and barr'd my castle door,
  The waves roll so gaily O,
Three summer days I grieved sore,
  Love me true!

For myself a day and night,
  The waves roll so gaily O,
And two to moan that lady bright,
  Love me true!

THISTLEDOWN.

(AN ENGLISH RURAL CUSTOM.)

LONG ago,—a little girl,
  Smooth of cheek and dark of curl,
  Like my daughter's nearly,—
I gather'd for my bridal bed
Many a hoary thistle-head
Before the flying tufts were shed,
  And saved them up so dearly.

O the happy days and dreams!
Endless Present,—lit with gleams
  Of a wondrous Future!

Day, and week, and month, and year,
Glide,—and what know you, my dear?
And what know I?   O little sphere
   Of every mortal creature!

Life has pleasure, life has pain,
Passing, not to come again,
   Blackest hours and brightest.
Time takes all things, all must go;
Byegones vanish—is it so?
Gone and lost for ever?—No!
   Not the least and lightest.

In Age, we laugh at dreams of Youth.
Are Age's dreams more like the truth?
   And what is life but feeling?
The world is something, none can doubt,
But no one finds its secret out;
To childhood, and to souls devout,
   Comes the best revealing.

Gay at heart are you, my child,
Gathering downy thistles wild;
   Cares nor fears oppress thee;
Gathering up, for joy, for moan,
When all these autumns, too, are flown,
The bed that you must lie upon.
   —God protect and bless thee!

WISHING.

(A CHILD'S SONG.)

Ring-Ting! I wish I were a Primrose,
A bright yellow Primrose blowing in the Spring!
    The stooping boughs above me,
    The wandering bee to love me,
  The fern and moss to creep across,
    And the Elm-tree for our king!

Nay—stay! I wish I were an Elm-tree,
A great lofty Elm-tree, with green leaves gay!
    The winds would set them dancing,
    The sun and moonshine glance in,
  The Birds would house among the boughs,
    And sweetly sing!

O—no! I wish I were a Robin,
A Robin or a little Wren, everywhere to go;
    Through forest, field, or garden,
    And ask no leave or pardon,
  Till Winter comes with icy thumbs
    To ruffle up our wing!

Well—tell! Where should I fly to,
Where go to sleep in the dark wood or dell?
    Before a day was over,
    Home comes the rover,
  For Mother's kiss,—sweeter this
    Than any other thing!

THE BIRD.

(A CHILD'S SONG.)

"BIRDIE, Birdie, will you pet?
   Summertime is far away yet.
You'll have silken quilts and a velvet bed,
And a pillow of satin for your head!"

"I'd rather sleep in the ivy wall;
No rain comes through, tho' I hear it fall;
The sun peeps gay at dawn of day,
And I sing, and wing away, away!"

"O Birdie, Birdie, will you pet?
Diamond-stones and amber and jet
We'll string for a necklace fair and fine,
To please this pretty bird of mine!"

"O thanks for diamonds, and thanks for jet,
But here is something daintier yet,—
A feather-necklace round and round,
That I wouldn't sell for a thousand pound!"

"O Birdie, Birdie, wont you pet?
We'll buy you a dish of silver fret,
A golden cup and an ivory seat,
And carpets soft beneath your feet!"

"Can running water be drunk from gold?
Can a silver dish the forest hold?
A rocking twig is the finest chair,
And the softest paths lie through the air,—
Goodbye, goodbye to my lady fair!"

HERE AND THERE.

(A JUVENILE CHORUS.)

[*One voice.*] WHERE'S LUCY? where's Lucy?
[*Two voices.*] Far, far in the wood;
[*Three or more voices.*] With wild birds for playmates,
And beech-nuts for food.

[*All.*] *No, here she is! here she is!*
Merry and gay,
With singing and ringing,
To join in our lay!

[*As before.*] Where's Henry? where's Henry?
He's out in the snow;
The stars shining keenly,
The cold wind doth blow.

No, here he is! &c.

Where's Julia? where's Julia?
  She's lost in the fog :
Go seek her, go find her,
  With man and with dog.

No, here she is ! &c.

Where's Herbert? where's Herbert?
  Poor Herbert's afloat;
The sea-waves all round him,
  High tossing his boat.

No, here he is ! &c.

Where's Charley? where's Charley?
  In China dwells he ;
He wears a long pigtail,
  Perpetually drinks tea.

No, here he is ! &c.

Where's Johnny? where's Johnny?
  In Nubia I know ;
He has climb'd a tall palm tree,—
  A lion's below.

No, here he is ! &c.

Where's Mary? where's Mary?
  Young Mary's asleep ;
And round her white pillow
  The little dreams creep.

No, here she is ! &c.

Where's Bertha? where's Bertha?
　　She has wings—she can fly;
She has flown to the bright moon—
　　Look up there and spy!

No, here she is! here she is!
　　Merry and gay,
With singing and ringing,
　　To join in our lay!

　　　[*Ad infinitum.*]

ROBIN REDBREAST.

(A CHILD'S SONG.)

GOODBYE, goodbye to Summer!
　　For Summer's nearly done;
The garden smiling faintly,
　　Cool breezes in the sun;
Our thrushes now are silent,
　　Our swallows flown away,—
But Robin's here, in coat of brown,
　　With ruddy breast-knot gay.
Robin, Robin Redbreast,
　　O Robin dear!
Robin sings so sweetly
　　In the falling of the year.

Bright yellow, red, and orange,
　　The leaves come down in hosts;

The trees are Indian Princes,
   But soon they'll turn to Ghosts;
The scanty pears and apples
   Hang russet on the bough;
Its Autumn, Autumn, Autumn late,
   'Twill soon be Winter now.
Robin, Robin Redbreast,
   O Robin dear!
And what will this poor Robin do?
   For pinching days are near.

The fireside for the cricket,
   The wheatstack for the mouse,
When trembling night-winds whistle
   And moan all round the house;
The frosty ways like iron,
   The branches plumed with snow,—
Alas! in Winter dead and dark
   Where can poor Robin go?
Robin, Robin Redbreast,
   O Robin dear!
And a crumb of bread for Robin,
   His little heart to cheer.

DOWN ON THE SHORE.

DOWN on the shore, on the sunny shore!
   Where the salt smell cheers the land;
Where the tide moves bright under boundless light,
   And the surge on the glittering strand;

Where the children wade in the **shallow** pools,
    Or run from the froth in play ;
Where the swift little boats with milk-white wings
    Are crossing the sapphire bay,
And the ship in full **sail,** with a fortunate gale,
    Holds proudly **on her way.**
Where the nets are spread **on** the grass **to dry,**
    And asleep, hard **by,** the fishermen **lie,**
Under the **tent** of the warm blue sky,
With **the** hushing wave on its golden floor
    To sing their lullaby.

Down on the shore, **on the stormy** shore !
    Beset by a growling **sea,**
Whose mad waves leap on the rocky steep
    Like wolves up a traveller's tree.
Where the foam flies wide, and an angry blast
    Blows the curlew **off, with a** screech ;
Where the brown **sea-wrack, torn up** by the roots,
    Is flung **out of fishes' reach ;**
Where the **tall** ship **rolls on the** hidden shoals,
    And scatters her planks on the beach.
Where slate and straw through the village spin,
And a cottage fronts the fiercest **din**
With **a** sailor's wife sitting **sad** within,
Hearkening the **wind and water's roar,**
    Till at last her tears begin.

THE DIRTY OLD MAN.

A LAY OF LEADENHALL.

IN a dirty old house lived a Dirty Old Man;
  Soap, towels, or brushes were not in his plan.
For forty long years, as the neighbours declared,
His house never once had been clean'd or repair'd.

'Twas a scandal and shame to the business-like street,
One terrible blot in a ledger so neat:
The shop full of hardware, but black as a hearse,
And the rest of the mansion a thousand times worse.

Outside, the old plaster, all spatter and stain,
Looked spotty in sunshine and streaky in rain;
The window-sills sprouted with mildewy grass,
And the panes from being broken were known to be
    glass.

On a ricketty signboard no learning could spell
The merchant who sold, or the goods he'd to sell;
But for house and for man a new title took growth,
Like a fungus,—the Dirt gave a name to them both.

Within, there were carpets and cushions of dust,
The wood was half rot, and the metal half rust,
Old curtains, half cobwebs, hung grimly aloof;
'Twas a Spiders' Elysium from cellar to roof.

There, king of the spiders, the Dirty Old Man
Lives busy and dirty as ever he can;
With dirt on his fingers and dirt on his face,
For the Dirty Old Man thinks the dirt no disgrace.

From his wig to his shoes, from his coat to his shirt,
His clothes are a proverb, a marvel of dirt;
The dirt is pervading, unfading, exceeding,—
Yet the Dirty Old Man has both learning and breeding.

Fine dames from their carriages, noble and fair,
Have enter'd his shop—less to buy than to stare;
And have afterwards said, though the dirt was so frightful,
The Dirty Man's manners were truly delightful.

Upstairs they don't venture, in dirt and in gloom,—
Mayn't peep at the door of the wonderful room
Such stories are told of, not half of them true;
The keyhole itself has no mortal seen through.

That room—forty years since, folk settled and deck'd it.
The luncheon's prepared, and the guests are expected
The handsome young host he is gallant and gay,
For his love and her friends will be with him to-day.

With solid and dainty the table is drest,
The wine beams its brightest, the flowers bloom their best;
Yet the host need not smile, and no guests will appear
For his sweetheart is dead, as he shortly shall hear.

Full forty years since, turn'd the key in that door.
'Tis a room deaf and dumb 'mid the city's uproar.
The guests, for whose joyance that table was spread,
May now enter as ghosts, for they're every one dead.

Through a chink in the shutter dim lights come and go;
The seats are in order, the dishes a-row;
But the banquet was wealth to the rat and the mouse
Whose descendants have long left the Dirty Old House.

Cup and platter are mask'd in thick layers of dust;
The flowers fall'n to powder, the wine swath'd in crust;
A nosegay was laid before one special chair,
And the faded blue ribbon that bound it lies there.

The old man has play'd out his parts in the scene.
Wherever he now is, I hope he's more clean.
Yet give we a thought free of scoffing or ban
To that Dirty Old House and that Dirty Old Man.

TWO FAIRIES IN A GARDEN.

" WHITHER goest, brother Elf?"

" The sun is weak—to warm myself
In a thick red tulip's core.
Whither thou?"

     " Till day be o'er,
To the dim and deep snow-palace
Of the closest lily-chalice,

Where is veil'd the light **of noon**
To be like my Lady's moon.
Thou art of the day, I ween?"

"Yet I not disown our Queen.
Nor at Lysc' am backward found
When the mighty feast comes round;
When She spreads abroad her power
To proclaim a midnight hour
For the pale **blue Fays** like thee
And the ruddy Elves like me
To mingle in a charmèd ring
With a perfect welcoming;
Guarded from the moon-stroke cold,
And wisp that scares **us** on the wold."

"Swift that Night **is** drawing near,
When your abrupt and jovial cheer
Mixes in our misty dance,
Meeting else by rarest chance.
We love dark undew'd recesses
Of the leafy wildernesses,
Or to hide in some cold flow'r
Shelter'd from the sunlight hour,
And more afflictive mortal eye."

"Gladly, gladly, do I **spy**
Human children playing nigh,
Feel, and so must you, **the grace**
Of a loving human face.
Else why come you in this place?

O my sister, if we might
Show ourselves to mortal sight
Far more often!—if they knew
Half the friendly turns we do!
Even now, a gentle thought
Would pay our service dimly wrought.
Paler favourites of the moon,
Can ye give or take such boon?"

"Chantings, brother, hear you might,
Softly sung through still of night;
Calling from the wëird North
Dreams like distant echoes forth,
Till through curtain'd shades they creep,
To inlay the gloomy floor of sleep
For babes, and souls that babe-like are:
So we bless them from afar
Like a faint but favouring star.
—But tell me how in fields or bowers
Thou hast spent these morning hours?"

"Through the tall hedge I have been,
Shadowy wall of crusted green,
Within whose heart the birds are seen.
Speeding swiftly thence away
To the crowning chestnut-spray,
I watch'd a tyrant steal along
Would slay the sweet thrush in her song;
Warn'd, she soon broke off from singing;
There we left the branchlet swinging.

Whispering robin, down the walk,
News of poising, pouncing hawk,
The sycamore I next must strew
On every leaf with honey dew.
And hither now from clouds I run;
For all my morning work is done."

"Alas, I wither in the sun,
Witless drawn to leave my nest
Ere the day be laid to rest!
But to-night we lightly troop
By the young moon's silver hoop;
Weaving wide our later ranks
As on evening river-banks
Shifting crowds of midges glance
Through mazes of their airy dance:
O might you come, O might you see
All our shadow'd revelry!
Yet the next night shall be rarer,
Next and next and next, still fairer
We are waxing every night,
Till our joy be full and bright;
Then as slowly do we wane
With gentle loss that makes no pain.
For thus are we with life endued:
Ye, I trow, have rougher food."

"Yes: with fragrant soul we're fed
Of every flower whose cheek is red,
Shunning yellow, blue, and white:
And southward go, at the nightingale's flight.

Many the faery nations be.
O! how I long, I long to see
The moonèd midnight of our feast
Flushing amber through the east,
When every cap in Elfendom
Into that great ring shall come,
Owf and Elf and Fairy blended,
Till th' imperial time be ended!
Even those fantastic Sprites
Lay aside their dear delights
Of freakish mischief and annoyance
In the universal joyance,
One of whom I saw of late
As I peep'd through window-grate,
(Under roof I may not enter)
Haunt the housewife to torment her;
Tangle up her skeins of silk,
Throw a mouse into her milk,
Hide her thimble, scorch her roast,
Quickly drive her mad almost;
And I too vex'd, because I would
Have brought her succour if I could.
—But where shall this be holden, say?
Far away?"

"O, far away.
Over river must we fly,
Over the sea, and the mountain high,
Over city, seen afar
Like a low and misty star,—

Soon beneath us glittering
Like million spark-worms.   But our wing
For the flight will ne'er suffice.
Some are training flitter-mice,
I a silver moth."

    " Be ware
How I'll thrid the vaulted air !
A dragon-fly with glassy wings,
Born beside the meadow springs,
That can arrow-swiftly glide
Thorough the glowing eventide,
Nor at twilight-fall grow slack,
Shall bear me on his long red back.
Dew-stars, meteors of the night,
May not strike him with affright,
He can needle through the wood,
That 's like a green earth-chainèd cloud,
Mountain-summits deftly rake,
Draw swift line o'er plain and lake,
If at Lysco I be last,
Other elves must journey fast.
Lu a vo !"

    " But Elf, I rede,
Of all your herbs take special heed.
Our Mistress tholes no garden flowers,
Though we have freedom of these bowers.
Tell me what you mean to treasure,
Each in 's atom ?"

"Gold-of-Pleasure,
Medic, Plumeseed, Fountain-arrow,
Vervain, Hungry-grass, and Yarrow,
Quatrefoil and Melilot."

"These are well. And I have got
Moonwort and the Filmy Fern,
Gather'd nicely on the turn.
Wo to fairy that shall bring
Bugloss for an offering,
Toad-flax, Barley of the Wall,
Enchanter's Nightshade, worst of all.
—Oh, brother, hush! I faint with fear!
A mortal footstep threatens near."

"None can see us, none can hear.
Yet, to make thee less afraid,
Hush we both as thou hast pray'd.
I will seek the verse to spell
Written round my dark flow'r's bell,
To sing at sunset. Fare-thee-well!"

THE BALLAD OF SQUIRE CURTIS.

A VENERABLE white-hair'd Man,
   A trusty man and true,
Told me this tale, as word for word
   I tell this tale to you.

Squire Curtis had a cruel mouth,
  Though honey was on his tongue;
Squire Curtis woo'd and wedded a wife,
  And she was fair and young.

But he said, "She cannot love me;
  She watches me early and late;
She is mild and good and cold of mood;"—
  And his liking turn'd to hate.

One autumn evening they rode through the woods,
  Far and far away;
"The dusk is drawing round," she said,
  "I fear we have gone astray."

He spake no word, but lighted down,
  And tied his horse to a tree;
Out of the pillion he lifted her;
  "'Tis a lonely place," said she.

Down a forest-alley he walk'd,
  And she walk'd by his side;
"Would Heav'n we were at home!" she said,
  "These woods are dark and wide!"

He spake no word, but still walk'd on;
  The branches shut out the sky;
In the darkest place he turn'd him round—
  "'Tis here that you must die."

Once she shriek'd and never again;
  He stabb'd her with his knife;
Once, twice, thrice, and every blow
  Enough to take a life.

A grave was ready; he laid her in;
  He fill'd it up with care;
Under the brambles and fallen leaves
  Small sign of a grave was there.

He rode for an hour at a steady pace,
  Till unto his house came he;
On face or clothing, on foot or hand,
  No stain that eye could see.

He boldly call'd to his serving-man,
  As he lighted at the door:
" Your Mistress is gone on a sudden journey,—
  May stay for a month or more.

" In two days I shall follow her;
  Let her waiting-woman know."
" Sir," said the serving-man, " My Lady
  Came in an hour ago."

Squire Curtis sat him down in a chair,
  And moved neither hand nor head.
In there came the waiting-woman,
  " Alas the day!" she said.

"Alas! good Sir," says the waiting-woman,
  "What aileth my Mistress dear,
That she sits alone without sign or word?
  There is something wrong, I fear!

" Her face was white as any corpse
  As up the stair she pass'd;
She never turn'd, she never spoke;
  And the chamber-door is fast.

"She's waiting for you." "A lie!" he shouts,
  And up to his feet doth start;
" My wife is buried in Brimley Holt,
  With three wounds in her heart."

They search'd the forest by lantern light,
  They search'd by dawn of day;
At noon they found the bramble-brake
  And the pit where her body lay.

They carried the murder'd woman home,
  Slow walking side by side.
Squire Curtis he swung upon gallows-tree,
  But confess'd before he died.

The venerable trusty Man
  With hair like drifted snow,
Told me this tale, as from his wife
  He learn'd it long ago.

"Her father, Sir, in early days,
　　Lived close by Curtis Hall;
Many's the time he heard folk tell
　　Of what did there befall.

"The story's true from first to last;
　　His name was Henry Dabb;
Died lammas last at eighty-four,—
　　You'll read it on the slab."

THE WONDROUS WELL.

CAME north and south and east and west,
　　Four Pilgrims to a mountain crest,
Each vow'd to search the wide world round,
Until the Wondrous Well be found;
For even here, as old songs tell,
Shine sun and moon upon that Well;
And now, the lonely crag their seat,
The water rises at their feet.

Said One, "This Well is small and mean,
Too petty for a village-green."
Another said, "So smooth and dumb—
From earth's deep centre can it come?"
The Third, "This water's nothing rare,
Hueless and savourless as air."
The Fourth, "A Fane I look'd to see:
Where the true Well is, *that* must be."

They rose and left the lofty crest,
One north, one south, one east, one west;
Through many seas and deserts wide
They wander'd, thirsting, till they died;
Because no other water can
Assuage the deepest thirst of man.
—Shepherds who by the mountain dwell,
Dip their pitchers in that Well.

THE MAIDS OF ELFIN-MERE.

'TWAS when the spinning-room was here.
   Came Three Damsels clothed in white,
With their spindles every night;
Two and one, and Three fair Maidens,
Spinning to a pulsing cadence,
Singing songs of Elfin-Mere;
Till the eleventh hour was toll'd,
Then departed through the wold.
    Years ago, and years ago;
    And the tall reeds sigh as the wind doth blow.

Three white Lilies, calm and clear,
And they were loved by every one;
Most of all, the Pastor's Son,
Listening to their gentle singing,
Felt his heart go from him, clinging
Round these Maids of Elfin-Mere;

Sued each night to make them stay,
Sadden'd when they went away.
 Years ago, and years ago;
 And the tall reeds sigh as the wind doth blow.

Hands that shook with love and fear
Dared put back the village clock,—
Flew the spindle, turn'd the rock,
Flow'd the song with subtle rounding,
Till the false "eleven" was sounding;
Then these Maids of Elfin-Mere
Swiftly, softly, left the room,
Like three doves on snowy plume.
 Years ago, and years ago;
 And the tall reeds sigh as the wind doth blow.

One that night who wander'd near
Heard lamentings by the shore,
Saw at dawn three stains of gore
In the waters fade and dwindle.
Nevermore with song and spindle
Saw we Maids of Elfin-Mere.
The Pastor's Son did pine and die;
Because true love should never lie.
 Years ago, and years ago;
 And the tall reeds sigh as the wind doth blow.

OLD MASTER GRUNSEY AND GOODMAN DODD.

STRATFORD-ON-AVON, A.D. 1597.

G OD save you, Goodman Dodd,—a sight to s
you!

D. Save you, good Master Grunsey,—Sir, how
you?

G. Middlish, thank heav'n. Rare weather for t
wheat.

D. Farms will be thirsty, after all this heat.

G. And so is we. Sit down on this here bench:
We'll drink a pot o'yaäl. Coom then, wench!
My service—ha! I'm well enough, i' fegs,
But for thir plaguey rheum i' both my legs.
Whiles I can't hardly get about: O dear!

D. You see, we don't get younger every year.

G. You're a young fellow yet.

D.   Well nigh three-sco

G. I be your elder fifteen year and more.
Hast any news?

D.   Not much. New Place be sold,
And Willy Shakespeare's bought it, so I'm told.

G. What, little Willy Shakespeare bought the Place !
Lord bless us, how young folk gets on apace !
Sir Hugh's girt house down by the grammar-school !—
This Shakespeare's (take my word upon't) no fool.
I minds him sin' he were so high's my knee ;
A gallows little chap as e'er ye see ;
One day I cotch'd him peltin' o' my geese
Below the church : " Yo let 'en swim i' peace,
" Yong dog !" I says, " or I shall fling 'ee in."
Will was on t'other bank, and did but grin,
And call out, "Sir, you come across to here !"

D. I knows old John this five and thirty year.
In old times many a cup he made me drink ;
But Willy warn't aborn then, I don't think,
Or might a' been a babe on's mother's arm,
When I did cart 'en fleeces from our farm.
I went a coortin' then, in Avon-Lane,
And, tho' bit furder, I was allays fain
To bring my cart thereby, upon a chance
To catch some foolish little nod or glance,
Or " meet me, Mary, won't 'ee, Charlcote way,
" Or down at Clopton Bridge, next holiday ?"—
Here *to* yer, maäster.

G.   Saäme to yo. 'Tis hot.
We might do wuss nor call another pot.
Good Mistress Nan !
               Will Shakespeare, troth, I knew ;
A nimble curly-pate and pretty too

About the street; he grow'd an idle lad,
And like enough, 'twas thought, to turn out bad;
I don't just fairly know, but folk did say
He vex'd the Lucys, and so fleed away.

   D. He's wuth as much as Tanner Twigg to-day;
And all by plays in Lunnon.

   G.   Folk talks big;
Will Shakespeare wuth as much as Tanner Twigg—
Tut tut! Be Will a player-man by trade?

   D. O' course he be, o' course he be; and made
A woundy heap o' money too, and bought
A playhouse for himsen like, out and out;
And makes up plays, beside, for 'en to act;
Tho' I cawn't tell 'ee rightly, for a fact,
If out o' books or's owan yead it be.
We'n other work to think on, yo and me.
They say Will's doin' foinely, howsomiver.

   G. Why, Dodd, the little chap were allays cliver.
I don't know nothing now o' such-like toys;
New fashions plenty, mun, sin' we war boys;
Mummins we used to han, wi' scriptur' hist'ries,
An' puppet-shows, an' moralties an' myst'ries;
The Death o' Judas was a pretty thing,
" Ju-dass! Ju-dass!" the Divil used to sing.
But time goes on, for sure, and fashion alters.

D. At th' Falcon, t'other night, says young Jack
    Walters,
" Willy's a great man now!"

G.   A jolterhead!
What does it count for, when all's done and said?
Ah! who'll obey, let Will say " Come " or " Go "?
Such-like as him don't reckon much, I trow.
Sir, they shall travel first, like thee and me,
See Lunnon, to find out what great men be.
Ay, marry, must they. Saints! to see the Court
Take water down to Greenwich; there's fine sport!
Her Highness i' her frills and puffs and pearls,
Barons, and lords, and chamberlains, and earls,
So thick as midges round her,—look at such
An' thou would'st talk of greatness! why, the touch
Be on their stewards and lackeys, Goodman Dodd,
Who'll hardly answer Shakespeare wi' a nod,
And let him come, doff'd cap and bended knee.
We knows a trifle, neighbour, thee and me.

D. We may, Sir. This here's grand old Stratford
    brew;
No better yaäl i' Lunnon, search it through.
New Place ben't no such bargain, when all's done;
'Twas dear, I knows it.

G.   Thou bought'st better, mun,
At Hoggin Fields: all ain't alike in skill.

D. Thanks to the Lord above! I've not done ill.
No more han yo, friend **Grunsey**, in yer trade.

G. So-so. But here's young Will wi' money made,
And money saved; whereon I sets him down,
Say else who likes, a credit to the town;
Tho' some do shake their yeads at player-folk.

D. A very civil man to chat and joke;
I've ofttimes had a bit o' talk wi' Will.

G. How doth old Master Shakespeare?

D. Bravely still.
And so doth madam too, the comely dame.

G. And Willy's wife—what used to be her name?
Older than Willy, six, seven year or so;
Ann something,—Hatchard was it? Hatchway?—no.

D. Why, Hathaway, fro' down by Shottery gate.
I don't think she's so much about o' late.
Their son, yo see, the only son they had,
Died last year, and she took on dreadful bad;
And so the fayther did awhile, I'm told.
This boy o' theirs was nine or ten year old.
—Willy himsen may bide here now, mayhap.

G. He allays were a cliver little chap.
I'm glad o's luck, an 'twere for old John's sake.
Your arm, sweet sir. Oh, how my legs do ache!

KING HENRY'S HUNT.

KING HENRY stood in Waltham Wood,
    One morn in merry May-time;
Years fifteen hundred thirty-six,
    From Christ, had roll'd away time.

King Henry stood in Waltham Wood,
    All young green, sunny-shady.
He would not mount his pawing horse,
    Though men and dogs were ready.

"What ails his Highness? Up and down
    In moody sort he paceth;
He is not wont to be so slack,
    Whatever game he chaseth."

He paced and stopp'd; he paced and turn'd;
    At times he inly mutter'd;
He pull'd his girdle, twitch'd his beard;
    But not one word he utter'd.

The hounds in couples nosed about,
    Or on the sward lay idle;
The huntsmen stole a fearful glance,
    While fingering girth or bridle.

Among themselves, but not too loud,
    The young lords laugh'd and chatter'd,
Or broke a branch of hawthorn-bloom,
    As though it nothing matter'd.

King Henry sat on a fell'd oak,
    With gloomier eyes and stranger;
His brows were knit, his lip he bit;
    To look that way was danger.

Mused he on Pope and Emperor?
    Denied them and defied them?
Or traitors in his very realm
    Complotting?—woe betide them!

Suddenly on the southern breeze,
    Distinct though distant, sounded
A cannon shot,—and to his feet
    The King of England bounded.

" My horse!" he shouts,—" Uncouple now!"
    And all were quickly mounted.
A hind was found; man, horse, and hound
    Like furious demons hunted.

Fast fled the deer by grove and glade,
    The chase did faster follow;
And every wild-wood alley rang
    With hunter's horn and hollo.

Away together stream'd the hounds;
    Forward press'd every rider.
You're free to slay a hind in May,
    If there's no calf beside her.

King Harry rode a mighty horse,
    His Grace being broad and heavy,
And like a stormy wind he crash'd
    Through copse and thicket leavy.

He rode so hard, and roar'd so loud,
    All men his course avoided;
The fiery steed, long held on fret,
    With many a snort enjoy'd it.

The hind was kill'd, and down they sat
    To flagon and to pasty.
" Ha, by Saint George, a noble Prince
    Tho' hot, by times, and hasty."

Lord Norfolk knew, and other few,
    Wherefore that chase began on
The signal of a gun far off,
    One growl of distant cannon,—

And why so jovial grew his Grace,
    That erst was sad and sullen.
With that boom from the Tower, had fall'n
    The head of fair Anne Bullen.

Her neck, which Henry used to kiss,
    The bloody axe did sever ;
Their little child, Elizabeth,
    She'll see no more for ever.

Gaily the King rides west away ;
    Each moment makes his glee more ;
To-morrow brings his wedding-day
    With beautiful Jane Seymour.

The sunshine falls, the wild-bird calls,
    Across the slopes of Epping ;
From grove to glade, through light and shade,
    The troops of deer are stepping.

KOSTAS.

A ROMAIC BALLAD.

SHE had nine noble brothers,
    This beautiful young Maid,
And of old gloomy Charon
    Not much was she afraid.

Young Kostas her betrothèd
    Of four estates was heir,
And for old gloomy Charon
    Right little did she care

Charon is the *Death* of the modern Greeks.

But Charon like a bird flew past,
  And shot his deathly dart,
Flew like a coal-black swallow,
  And pierced her to the heart.

Then deep, deep did her father sigh,
  And loud her mother moan,
"O my one only daughter,
  My fair, my only one!"

And down the valley Kostas came,
  With twice three hundred men,
And sixty-two musicians,
  Along the mountain glen.

" Oh! stop the marriage jubilee,
  Musicians, play no more;
Oh, stop awhile, for I can see
  A cross upon the door.

"It may be one of her brethren
  Lies wounded on his bed;
Perchance her old grandfather
  Is dying now, or dead."

He spurreth to the churchyard
  His steed so black and brave,
And there he finds the sacristan
  Digging in a grave.

"O Sacristan, I greet thee!
  For whom that grave?" he cries.
"'Tis for a fair young Maiden,
  Her with the beautiful eyes;

"Who had nine noble brethren
  Within her father's gates,
And Kostas for her bridegroom,
  The heir of four estates."

"O Sacristan, I pray thee,
  Now dig the grave more wide,
Now dig it wide enough for two
  To rest there side by side."

He drew his golden-hilted sword,
  He plunged it in his breast;
And there the young betrothèd lie
  Side by side at rest.

EMILY.

"GOOD evening. Why, of course it's you!
  You 'half imagined,'—O I knew!
There, there, don't make a fuss, my dear,
Come in and let's have supper here.

"You're married now, George; yes, I heard
And looking bright, upon my word

And I?—a little thin or so?—
One can't make cottage-roses grow
As well in London—O dear me!
But never mind; it's life, you see.

" Her name—don't tell me; I don't care.
Of course you make a loving pair.
Your jolly healths! Why, there you sit,
And never eat or drink a bit.
' How well I'm drest '—you think so, eh?
You like my hair done up this way?

" Oh don't go yet, George! stay, do stay!
Five minutes longer! please don't go!
I'm not fit company, I know—
But just this one time—just this last!

" D'ye ever think of days gone past,
When you and I a-courting went,
So loving, and so innocent?
Our walks, our little messages,
Our notes, our quarrels; after these,
Our makings-up—O were we not
Rare fools? Then, of a sudden, came
The desperate quarrel, and for what?
For nothing! I was most to blame.

" What use in crying? Ain't it funny?
Nay, my good sir, I don't want money.
I don't, George; no, I don't indeed.
Why, I can lend you if you need.

Stop, I'll take this; I'll tell you why;
A little locket I shall buy,
(Now mayn't I?) big enough to hold
A lock of hair, that you forgot,
And so I kept it back.

      " How cold
The night-air strikes when one's so hot!
Ah, you won't kiss me now. All right,
Ta ta, George; off you go; good-night!"

THE SHOOTING STAR.

AUTUMNAL night's deep azure dome
 Darken'd the lawn and terrace high,
Where groups had left their music-room
 For starry hush and open sky,
To watch the meteors, how they went
Across the stately firmament.

As Walter paced with Josephine,
 The loveliest maid of all he knew,
Touch'd by the vast and shadowy scene,
 Their friendly spirits closer drew,
Beneath the dim-lit hollow night,
And those strange signals moving bright.

" A wish," said Walter,—" have you heard—
 Wish'd in the shooting of a star,
Fulfils itself?" " Prepare your word,"
 Said Josephine; " there's nought to mar

The shining chance." "And may I tell?"
"O no! for that would break the spell."

But now a splendid meteor flew,
    And ere it died the wish was made,
And won: for in a flash they knew
    The happy truth, so long delay'd,
Which months and years had never brought,—
From this bright fleeting moment caught.

LADY ALICE.

I.

NOW what doth Lady Alice so late on the turret stair,
Without a lamp to light her, but the diamond in her hair;
When every arching passage overflows with shallow gloom,
And dreams float through the castle, into every silent room?

She trembles at her footsteps, although they fall so light;
Through the turret loopholes she sees the wild midnight;
Broken vapours streaming across the stormy sky;
Down the empty corridors the blast doth moan and cry.

She steals along a gallery; she pauses by a door;
And fast her tears are dropping down upon the oaken
    floor;
And thrice she seems returning—but thrice she turns
    again :—
How heavy lies the cloud of sleep on that old father's
    brain!

Oh, well it were that *never* shouldst thou waken from
    thy sleep!
For wherefore should they waken, who waken but to
    weep?
No more, no more beside thy bed doth Peace a vigil
    keep,
But Woe,—a lion that awaits thy rousing for its leap.

II.

An afternoon of April, no sun appears on high,
But a moist and yellow lustre fills the deepness of the
    sky:
And through the castle-gateway, left empty and forlorn
Along the leafless avenue an honour'd bier is borne.

They stop. The long line closes up like some gigantic
    worm;
A shape is standing in the path, a wan and ghost-like
    form,
Which gazes fixedly; nor moves, nor utters any sound
Then, like a statue built of snow, sinks down upon the
    ground.

And though her clothes are ragged, and though her
   feet are bare,
And though all wild and tangled falls her heavy silk-
   brown hair;
Though from her eyes the brightness, from her cheeks
   the bloom is fled,
They know their Lady Alice, the darling of the dead.

With silence, in her own old room the fainting form
   they lay,
Where all things stand unalter'd since the night she
   fled away :
But who—but who—shall bring to life her father from
   the clay?
But who shall give her back again her heart of a former
   day?

THE TOUCHSTONE.

A MAN there came, whence none can tell,
   Bearing a Touchstone in his hand;
And tested all things in the land
By its unerring spell.

Quick birth of transmutation smote
   The fair to foul, the foul to fair;
   Purple nor ermine did he spare,
Nor scorn the dusty coat.

Of heirloom jewels, prized so much,
    Were many changed to chips and clods,
    And even statues of the Gods
Crumbled beneath its touch.

Then angrily the people cried,
    "The loss outweighs the profit far;
    Our goods suffice us as they are;
We will not have them tried."

And since they could not so prevail
    To check his unrelenting quest,
    They seized him, saying—"Let him test
How real it is, our jail!"

But, though they slew him with the sword,
    And in a fire his Touchstone burn'd,
    Its doings could not be o'erturn'd,
Its undoings restored.

And when, to stop all future harm,
    They strew'd its ashes on the breeze;
    They little guess'd each grain of these
Convey'd the perfect charm.

North, south, in rings and amulets,
    Throughout the crowded world 'tis borne;
    Which, as a fashion long outworn,
Its ancient mind forgets.

A WIFE.

THE wife sat thoughtfully turning over
   A book inscribed with the school-girl's name,
A tear, one tear, fell hot on the cover
   So quickly closed when her husband came.

He came and he went away, it was nothing;
   With commonplace words upon either side;
But, just with the sound of the room-door shutting,
   A dreadful door in her soul stood wide.

Love she had read of in sweet romances,
   Love that could sorrow, but never fail;
Built her own palace of noble fancies,
   All the wide world like a fairy-tale.

Bleak and bitter and utterly doleful
   Spread to this woman her map of life:
Hour after hour she look'd in her soul, full
   Of deep dismay and turbulent strife.

Face in hands, she knelt on the carpet;
   The cloud was loosen'd, the storm-rain fell.
O! life has so much to wilder and warp it,
   One poor heart's day what poet could tell?

THE OLD SEXTON.

(INSCRIBED TO ALFRED RETHEL.)

'TWAS nigh the hour of evening pray'r;
  The Sexton climb'd his turret-stair,
Wearily, being very old.
The wind of Spring blew fresh and cold,
Wakening there Æolian thrills,
And carrying fragrance from the hills.

Through a carven cleft he lean'd,
Eyeing the landscape newly green'd;
The large sun, slowly moving down,
Flush'd the chimneys of the town,—
The same where he was first alive
Eighty years ago and five.

Babe he sees himself, and boy;
Youth, astir with hope and joy;
Wife and wedded love he sees;
Children's children round his knees;
Friends departing one by one;
The graveyard in the setting sun.

He seats him in a stony niche;
The bell-rope sways within his reach;
High in the rafters of the roof
The metal warder hangs aloof;
All the townsfolk wait to hear
That voice they know this many a year.

It is past the ringing hour;
There is silence in the tower;
Save that on a pinnacle
A robin sits, and sings full well.
Hush—at length for prayer they toll:
God receive the parted soul!

THE FAITHLESS KNIGHT.

IT is a careless pretty may, down by yon river-side;
Her face, the whole world's pleasure, she gladly hath espied;
And tossing back her golden hair, her singing echoes wide;
When gaily to the grassy shore a youthful knight doth ride.

And vaulting from his courser, that stoops the head to drink,
And greeting well the Maiden fair, by running water's brink,
He throws about her slender neck a chain of costly link:
Too courteous he for glamourie, as any may might think.

All through the flowery meadows, in the summer evening warm,
The rippling river murmurs low, the dancing midges swarm;
But far away the pretty may, nor makes the least alarm,
Sits firm on lofty saddle-bow, within the young knight's arm.

Now months are come, and months are gone, with sun
    shine, breeze, and rain;
The song on grassy river-shore you shall not hear again
The proud knight spurs at tournament, in Germany o
    Spain,
Or sues in silken bow'r to melt some lady's high dis
    dain.

And thus in idle hour he dreams—" I've wander'd eas
    and west;
I've whisper'd love in many an ear, in earnest or in jest
That summer day—that pretty may—perhaps sh
    loved me best?
I recollect her face, methinks, more often than the rest.

THE MOWERS.

WHERE mountains round a lonely dale
    Our cottage-roof enclose,
Come night or morn, the hissing pail
    With fragrant cream o'erflows;
And roused at break of day from sleep,
    And cheerly trudging hither,—
A scythe-sweep, and a scythe-sweep,
    We mow the grass together.

The fog drawn up the mountain-side
    And scatter'd flake by flake,
The chasm of blue above grows wide,
    And richer blue the lake;

Gay sunlights o'er the hillocks creep,
   And join for golden weather,—
A scythe-sweep, and a scythe-sweep,
   We mow the dale together.

The goodwife stirs at five, we know,
   The master soon comes round,
And many swaths must lie a-row
   Ere breakfast-horn shall sound;
Sweet vernal-grass, and foxtail deep,
   The spike or silvery feather,—
A scythe-sweep, and a scythe-sweep,
   We mow them down together.

The noon-tide brings its welcome rest
   Our toil-wet brows to dry;
Anew with merry stave and jest
   The shrieking hone we ply.
White falls the brook from steep to steep
   Among the purple heather,—
A scythe-sweep, and a scythe-sweep,
   We mow the dale together.

For dial, see, our shadows turn;
   Low lies the stately mead:
A scythe, an hour-glass, and an urn—
   All flesh is grass, we read.
To-morrow's sky may laugh or weep,
   To Heav'n we leave it whether:
A scythe-sweep, and a scythe-sweep,
   We've done our task together.

WINDLASS SONG.

HEAVE at the windlass!—Heave O, cheerly, men!
  Heave all at once, with a will!
    The tide quickly making,
    Our cordage a-creaking,
  The water has put on a frill,
            Heave O!

Fare you well, sweethearts!—Heave O, cheerly, men!
  Fare you well, frolic and sport!
    The good ship all ready,
    Each dog-vane is steady,
  The wind blowing dead out of port,
            Heave O!

Once in blue water—Heave O, cheerly, men!
  Blow it from north or from south;
    She'll stand to it tightly,
    And curtsey politely,
  And carry a bone in her mouth,
            Heave O!

Short cruise or long cruise—Heave O, cheerly, men!
  Jolly Jack Tar thinks it one.
    No latitude dreads he
    Of White, Black, or Red sea,
  Great icebergs, or tropical sun,
            Heave O!

One other turn, and Heave O, cheerly, men!
Heave, and goodbye to the shore!
Our money, how went it?
We shared it and spent it;
Next year we'll come back with some more,
Heave O!

HOMEWARD BOUND.

HEAD the ship for England!
Shake out every sail!
Blithe leap the billows,
Merry sings the gale.
Captain, work the reck'ning;
How many knots a day?—
Round the world and home again,
That's the sailor's way!

We've traded with the Yankees,
Brazilians, and Chinese;
We've laugh'd with dusky beauties
In shade of tall palm-trees;
Across the Line and Gulf-stream—
Round by Table Bay—
Everywhere and home again,
That's the sailor's way!

Nightly stands the North Star
Higher on our bow;
Straight we run for England;
Our thoughts are in it now.

Jolly time with friends ashore,
  When we've drawn our pay!—
All about and home again,
  That's the sailor's **way**!

Tom will to his parents,
  Jack will to his dear,
Joe to wife and children,
  Bob to pipes and **beer**;
Dicky to the dancing-room,
  To hear the fiddles **play**;—
Round the world and home again,
  That's the sailor's way!
*Round the world and home again,
  That's the sailor's way!*

THE SAILOR.

A ROMAIC BALLAD.

THOU that hast a daughter
  For one to woo and wed,
Give her to a husband
  With snow upon his head;
Oh, give her to an old man,
  Though little **joy** it be,
Before the best young **sailor**
  That sails upon the sea!

How luckless is the sailor
  When sick and **like to die**!

He sees no tender mother,
  No sweetheart standing by.
Only the captain speaks to him,—
  Stand up, stand up, young man
And steer the ship to haven,
  As none beside thee can.

Thou sayst to me, "Stand up, stand up;"
  I say to thee, take hold,
Lift me a little from the deck,
  My hands and feet are cold.
And let my head, I pray thee,
  With handkerchiefs be bound;
There, take my love's own handkerchief,
  And tie it tightly round.

Now bring the chart, the doleful chart;
  See, where these mountains meet—
The clouds are thick around their head,
  The mists around their feet:
Cast anchor here; 'tis deep and safe
  Within the rocky cleft;
The little anchor on the right,
  The great one on the left.

And now to thee, O captain,
  Most earnestly I pray,
That they may never bury me
  In church or cloister gray;—

But on the windy sea-beach,
   At the ending of the land,
All on the surfy sea-beach,
   Deep down into the sand.

For there will come the sailors,
   Their voices I shall hear,
And at casting of the anchor
   The yo-ho loud and clear;
And at hauling of the anchor
   The yo-ho and the cheer,—
Farewell, my love, for to thy bay
   I nevermore may steer!

THE PILOT BOAT.

I.

A SCHOONER's in the bay,
   With a signal at her fore;
And I heard the Pilot say—
  "Tho' a squall may come to-night,
  We shall get on board all right,
And the tide begins to flow at break of day."
  "Shove her off, my lad," cries he,
  "We've a craft that's fit for sea!"
And the ripples on the shore
Murmur softly as they run
Through the crimson evening light,
While the father and the son
         Sail away.

II.

When cliff and wave grow dark,
   Shines a cottage by the strand
With its feeble taper-spark,
   Where the Pilot's wife is sewing
   Whilst her little children sleep;
All the gloomy heav'n above no glimmer showing.
     Ha!—lightning!—and a crash
       Like the downfall of the skies;
   Rushing rain, booming Deep,
   Sudden gale with fury blowing.
   Out of nothing, at each flash
       Leap the dreadful sea and land.
   Was that wind she heard? or—hark!
            Shouts and cries?

III.

A morn remorseful, pale,
   For the frenzy overpast,—
A sullen sinking gale,—
   Flying clouds, torn and shatter'd,
And a dismal gleam of day through them cast
     On the wilderness in motion
     Of the ghastly rugged ocean
       With its dull unceasing roar,
     And the birds that scream and flee,
       And the misty wreck-strewn shore,
     And a black unmoving Boat
       Flung keel upwards, bruised and batter'd,
         Past the help of sail or oar:

But the Pilot, stout and steady,
And his Boy, brave and ready,—
On what voyage, on what sea,
Do they float?

NANNY'S SAILOR LAD.

NOW fare-you-well! my bonny ship,
For I am for the shore.
The wave may flow, the breeze may blow,
They'll carry me no more.

And all as I came walking
And singing up the sand,
I met a pretty maiden,
I took her by the hand.

But still she would not raise her head,
A word she would not speak,
And tears were on her eyelids,
Dripping down her cheek.

Now grieve you for your father?
Or husband might it be?
Or is it for a sweetheart
That's roving on the sea?

It is not for my father,
I have no husband dear,
But oh! I had a sailor lad
And he is lost, I fear.

Three long years
  I am grieving for his sake,
And when the stormy wind blows loud,
  I lie all night awake.

I caught her in my arms,
  And she lifted up her eyes,
I kiss'd her ten times over
  In the midst of her surprise.

Cheer up, cheer up, my Nanny,
  And speak again to me;
O dry your tears, my darling,
  For I'll go no more to sea.

I have a love, a true true love,
  And I have golden store,
The wave may flow, the breeze may blow,
  They'll carry me no more!

CAPE USHANT.[1]

(THE LAST LOOK.)

OUR ship, the stout Bellerophon,
  Off Rochefort Harbour lay:
We took a passenger on board,
  And slowly sail'd away.
Seven days and nights, with baffling winds,
  We strove to fetch Tor Bay.

---

[1] The facts given by a midshipman of the "Bellerophon." See Notes.

The eighth day, with the rising sun,
  A morning in July,
French land upon our starboard bow
  We plainly could descry;

When I, a little middy,
  (Ah! sixty years ago)
Came up, to take my watch on deck,
  Into the early glow.

Magnificently rose the sun
  Above the hills of France,
And spread his splendour on the sea,
  And through the sky's expanse.

Meanwhile, upon the poop, alone,
  Our Passenger stood there,
And view'd the gently gliding land
  In clearest morning air,—
The cliffs of Ushant, and the slopes
  Of shadowy Finisterre.

" Ushant?" he ask'd,—and I replied,
  " Yes, sire." Whereon he raised
His little pocket-telescope,
  And gazed, and ever gazed.

For hours and hours he hardly moved;
  And if his eyes grew dim,
We never saw it; there he stood,
  And none went near to him.

Till with a faint and fickle wind
    We drew from off the coast,
And in a noontide haze of heat
    France faded, and was lost.

Napoleon's thoughts in that last look
    It were in vain to seek;
He had enough to think upon
    If he had gazed a week.

And sometimes from his rock, perhaps,
    He saw, amid the shine
Of lonely waves, Cape Ushant's ghost
    Far on the dim sea-line.

CIVITAS DEI.

I.

THE roads are long and rough, with many a bend,
        But always tend
  To that Eternal City, and the home
Of all our footsteps, let them haste or creep.
    That city is not Rome.
   Great Rome is but a heap
    Of shards and splinters lying in a field;
      Where children of to-day
     Among the fragments play,
And for themselves in turn new cities build.

II.

That city's gates and towers,
Superber than the sunset's cloudy crags,
Know nothing of the earth's all-famous flags;
  It hath its own wide region, its own air.
    Our kings, our lords, our mighty warriors,
      Are not known there.
        The wily pen, the cannon's fierce report,
          Fall very short.

III.

    Where is it? . . . Tell who can.
Ask all the best geographers' advice.
'Tis builded in no valley of Japan
  Or secret Africa, nor isle unfound
As yet, nor in a region calm and warm
    Enclosed from every storm
  Within the magical and monstrous bound
    Of polar ice.

IV.

    Where is it? . . . Who can tell?
      Yet surely know,
Whatever land or city you may claim
    And count as yours—
    From otherwhere you came,
      Elsewhither you must go;
Ev'n to a City with foundations low
  As Hell, with battlements Heaven-high,
Which is eternal; and its place and name
    Are mystery.

STORIES.

THE MUSIC-MASTER.

A LOVE STORY.

PART I.

I.

MUSIC and Love!—If lovers hear me sing,
  I will for them essay the simple tale,
To hold some fair young listeners in a ring
  With echoes gathered from an Irish vale,
Where still, methinks, abide my golden years,
Though I not with them,—far discern'd through tears.

II.

When evening fell upon the village-street
  And brother fields, reposing hand in hand,
Unlike where flaring cities scorn to meet
  The kiss of dusk that quiets all the land,
'Twas pleasant laziness to loiter by
Houses and cottages, a friendly spy.

III.

And hear the frequent fiddle that would glide
  Through jovial mazes of a jig or reel,
Or sink from sob to sob with plaintive slide,
  Or mount the steps of swift exulting zeal;
For our old village was with music fill'd
Like any grove where thrushes wont to build.

IV.

Mixt with the roar of bellows and of flame,
   Perhaps the reed-voice of a clarionet
From forge's open ruddy shutter came;
   Or round some hearth were silent people set,
Where the low flute, with plaintive quivering, ran on
Through "Colleen Dhas" or "Hawk of Ballyshannon."

V.

Or pictured on those bygone, shadowy nights
   I see a group of girls at needlework,
Placed round a candle throwing soft half-lights
   On the contrasted faces, and the dark
And fair-hair'd heads, a bunch of human flow'rs;
And many a ditty cheers th' industrious hours.

VI.

Pianoforte's sound from curtain'd pane
   Would join the lofty to the lowly roof
In the sweet links of one harmonious chain;
   And often down the street some Glee's old woof,
" Hope of my heart "—" Ye Shepherds "—" Lightly
    tread,"
Would mesh my steps or wrap me in my bed.

VII.

The most delicious chance, if we should hear,
   Pour'd from our climbing glen's enfoliaged rocks,
At dusk some solitary bugle, clear,
   Remote, and melancholy; echo mocks
The strain delighted, wafting it afar
Up to the threshold of the evening star.

VIII.

And Gerald was our music-master's name;
  Young Gerald White; whose mother, not long wed,
Only to make him ours by birthright came.
  Her *Requiescat* I have often read,
Where thickest ivy hangs its ancient pall
Over the dumb and desolate abbey wall.

IX.

The father found a music-pupil rare,
  More ready still to learn than he to teach;
His art no longer was his only care,
  But now young Gerald with it, each for each;
And with a secret and assiduous joy
The grave musician taught his happy boy.

X.

The boy's whole thought to Music lean'd and sway'd;
  He heard a minor in the wind at night,
And many a tune the village noises play'd;
  The thunder roar'd like bands before the might
Of marching armies; in deep summer calm
The falling brooklet would intone a psalm.

XI.

The Chapel organ-loft, his father's seat,
  Was to the child his earthly paradise;
And that celestial one that used to greet
  His infant dreams, could take no other guise
Than visions of green curtains and gold pipes,
And angels of whom quire-girls were the types.

XII.

Their fresh young voices from the congregation,
  Train'd and combined by simple rules of chant,
And lifted on the harmonious modulation
  Roll'd from the lofty organ, ministrant
To sacred triumph, well might bring a thought
Of angels there,—perhaps themselves it brought.

XIII.

Poor girls the most were: this one had her nest,
  A mountain mavis, in the craggy furze;
Another in close lane must toil and rest,
  And never cage-bird's song more fine than hers,
Humming at work all through the busy week,
Set free in Sunday chorus, proud and meek.

XIV.

And when young Gerald might adventure forth
  Through Music-land,—where hope and memory
And singing fly beyond the bourne of earth,
  And the whole spirit full of aching bliss
Would follow as the parting shrouds reveal
Glimpses ineffable, but soon conceal,—

XV.

While all the hills, mayhap, and distant plain,
  Village and brook were shaded, fold on fold,
With the slow dusk, and on the purpling pane
  Soft twilight barr'd with crimson and with gold
Lent to that simple little house of prayer
A richly solemn, a cathedral air;

XVI.

His symphonies to suit the dying close
   Suffused it with a voice that could not ask
In vain for tears; not ask in vain from those
   Who in the dew fulfill'd their pious task,
Kneeling with rosaries beside a grave;
To whom a heavenly comforting it gave.

XVII.

Thus village years went by. Day after day
   Flow'd, as a stream unvext with storms or floods
Flows by some islet with a hawthorn gray;
   Where circling seasons bring a share of buds,
Nests, blossoms, ruddy fruit,—and, in their turn,
Of withering leaves and frosty twigs forlorn.

XVIII.

So went the years, that never may abide;
   Boyhood to manhood, manly prime to age,
Ceaselessly gliding on, as still they glide;—
   Until the father yields for heritage
(Joyful, yet with a sigh) the master's place
To Gerald—who could higher fortune grace.

XIX.

But the shy youth has yet his hours of leisure:
   And now, the Spring upon the emerald hills
Dancing with flying clouds, how keen his pleasure,
   Plunged in deep glens or tracking upland rills,
Till lessening light recal him from his roaming
To breathe his gather'd secrets to the gloaming.

XX.

Spring was around him, and within him too.
  Delightful season!—life without a spur
Bounds gaily forward, and the heart is new
  As the green wand fresh budded on a fir;
And Nature, into jocund chorus waking,
Bids every young voice to her merry-making.

XXI.

Gerald, high echoing this delightful Spring,
  Pour'd from his finger-tips electric power
In audible creations swift of wing,
  Till sunshine glimpsing through an April shower,
And clouds, and delicate glories, and the bound
Of lucid sky came melting into sound.

XXII.

Our ear receives in common with our eye
  One Beauty, flowing through a different gate,
With melody its form, and harmony
  Its hue; one mystic Beauty is the mate
Of Spirit indivisible, one love
Her look, her voice, her memory do move.

XXIII.

Yet sometimes in his playing came a tone
  Not learn'd of sun or shadow, wind or brook,
But thoughts so much his own he dared not own,
  Nor, prizing much, appraise them; dared not lo⟨ok⟩
In fear to lose an image undefined
That brighten'd every vista of his mind.

XXIV.

Two pupils dwelt upon the river-side,
  At Cloonamore, a cottage near the rush
Of narrow'd waters breaking from a wide
  And pond-like smoothness, brimming green and flush
On dark groves; here for Gerald, truth to say,
His weekly task was more than holiday.

XXV.

A quiet home it was; compact and neat
  As a wren's nest. A gentle woman's choice
Had built and beautified the green retreat;
  But in her labours might she not rejoice,
Being call'd away to other place of rest;
And spent her last breath in a dear behest.

XXVI.

That was for her two daughters: she had wed
  A plain, rough husband, though a kind and true;
And "Dearest Bernard," from her dying bed
  She whisper'd, "Promise me you'll try to do
For Ann and Milly what was at my heart,
If God had spared me to perform my part."

XXVII.

As well as no abundant purse allow'd,
  Or as the neighbouring village could supply,
The father kept his promise, and was proud
  To see the girls grow up beneath his eye
Two ladies in their culture and their mien;
Though not the less there lay a gulf between.

XXVIII.

A spirit unrefined the elder had,
  An envious eye, a tongue of petty scorn.
That women these may own—how true! how sad!
  And these, though Ann had been a countess born,
Had mark'd her meaner to the dullest sight
Than stands a yellow lily with a white.

XXIX.

White lily,—Milly,—darling little girl!
  I think I see as once I saw her stand;
Her soft hair waving in a single curl
  Behind her ear; a kid licking her hand;
Her fair young face with health and racing warm,
And loose frock blown about her slender form.

XXX.

The dizzy lark, a dot on the white cloud,
  That sprinkles music to the vernal breeze,
Was not more gay than Milly's joyous mood;
  The silent lark that starry twilight sees
Cradled among the braird in closest bower,
Not more quiescent than her tranquil hour.

XXXI.

Her mind was open, as a flowery cup
  That gathers richness from the sun and dew,
To knowledge, and as easily drew up
  The wholesome sap of life; unwatch'd it grew,
A lovely blossom in a shady place;
And like her mind, so was her innocent face.

XXXII.

At all times fair, it never look'd so fair
　　As when the holy glow of harmonies
Lighted it through ; her spirit as it were
　　An azure heav'n outshining at her eyes ;
With Gerald's tenor, while the fountain sprung
Of her contralto, fresh and pure and young.

XXXIII.

In years a child when lessons thus began,
　　Child is she still, yet nearly woman grown ;
For childhood stays with woman more than man,
　　In voice and cheek and mouth, nor these alone ;
And up the sky with no intense revealing
May the great dawn of womanhood come stealing.

XXXIV.

Now must the moon of childhood, trembling white,
　　Faint in the promise of the flushing heaven ;
Looks are turn'd eastward, where new orient light
　　Suffuses all the air with subtle leaven ;
And shadowy mountain-paths begin to show
Their unsuspected windings 'mid the glow.

XXXV.

Her silky locks have ripen'd into brown,
　　Her soft blue eyes grown deeper and more shy,
And lightly on her lifted head the crown
　　Of queenly maidenhood sits meek and high ;
Her frank soul lives in her ingenuous voice,
Most purely tuned to sorrow or rejoice.

XXXVI.

Within the chapel on a Sunday morn
   She bows her mild head near the altar-rail,
And raises up that mild full voice unworn
   Into the singing ;—should a Sunday fail,
There's one would often mark her empty seat,
There's one would find their anthem incomplete.

XXXVII.

Few her companions are, and few her books ;
   And in a ruin'd convent's circling shade,
The loveliest of tranquil river-nooks,
   Where trailing birch, fit bow'r for gentle maid,
And feather'd fir-tree half shut out the stream,
She often sits alone to read or dream.

XXXVIII.

Sometimes through leafy lattice she espies
   A flitting figure on the other shore ;
But ever past th' enchanted precinct hies
   That wanderer, and where the rapids roar
Through verdured crags, shelters his beating heart,
Foolishly bent to seek, yet stay apart.

XXXIX.

Then Milly can resume her reverie,
   About a real friend, one that she could love ;
But finds her broken thought is apt to flee
   To what seem other musings ; slowly move
The days, and counted days move ever slowest :
Milly ! how long ere thy own heart thou knowest ?

XL.

Sooner than Gerald his. His path-side birds
  Are scarcely more unconscious or more shrinking.
Yet would he tell his love in simple words
  Did love stand clearly in his simple thinking.
High the discovery, and too high for one
Who counts his life as though not yet begun.

XLI.

For all the rest seem sage and busy men;
  And he alone despised, and justly too,
Or borne with merely;—could he venture then
  To deem this rich inheritance his due?
Slowly the fine and tender soul discerns
Its rareness, and its lofty station learns.

XLII.

And now, 'tis on a royal eventide
  When the ripe month sets glowing earth and air,
And Summer by a stream or thicket-side
  Twists amber honeysuckles in her hair,—
Gerald and Milly meet by trembling chance,
And step for step are moving, in a trance.

XLIII.

Their pathway foliage-curtain'd and moss-grown:
  Behind the trees the white flood flashing swift,
Through many moist and ferny rocks flung down,
  Roars steadily, where sunlights play and shift:
How oft they stop, how long, they nothing know,
Nor how the pulses of the evening go.

XLIV.

Their talk?—the dappled hyacinthine glade
   Lit up in points of blue,—how soft and treble
The kine's deep lowing is **by** distance made,—
   The quail's "twit-wit-wit," like a hopping pebble
Thrown along ice,—the dragonflies, the birds,
The rustling twig,—all noticed in **few words.**

XLV.

A level pond, inlaid with lucid shadows
   Of groves and crannied cliffs and evening sky,
And rural domes of hay, where the green meadows
   Slope to embrace its margin peacefully,
The slumb'ring river to the rapid draws;
And here, upon a grassy jut, they **pause.**

XLVI.

How **shy** a strength **is Love's,** that so much fears
   Its darling secret to itself **to own!**
Their rapt, illimitable mood **appears**
   A beauteous miracle for each alone;
Exalted high above all range of hope
By the pure soul's eternity **of scope.**

XLVII.

Yet in both hearts a prophecy is breathed
   Of how this evening's phantom may arise,
In richer hues than ever sunlight wreathed
   On hill or wood or wave: in brimming eyes
The glowing landscape melts away from each;
And full their bosoms swell, too full for speech.

XLVIII.

Is it a dream? The countless happy stars
   Stand silently into the deepening blue;
In slow procession all the molten bars
   Of cloud move down; the air is dim with dew;
Eve scatters roses on the shroud of day;
The common world sinks far and far away.

XLIX.

With goodnight kiss the zephyr, half asleep,
   Sinks to its cradle in the dusk of trees,
Where river-chimings tolling sweet and deep
   Make lullaby, and all field-scents that please
The Summer's children float into the gloom
Dream-interwoven in a viewless loom.

L.

Clothed with an earnest paleness, not a blush,
   And with th' angelic gravity of love,
Each lover's face amid the twilight hush
   Is like a saint's whose thoughts are all above
In perfect gratitude for heavenly boon;
And o'er them for a halo comes the moon.

LI.

Thus through the leaves and the dim dewy croft
   They linger homeward. Flowers around their feet
Bless them, and in the firmament aloft
   Night's silent ardours. And an hour too fleet,
Though stretching years from all the life before,
Conducts their footsteps to her cottage door.

LII.

Thenceforth they meet more timidly?—in truth,
    Some lovers might, but all are not the same;
In the clear ether of their simple youth
    Steady and white **ascends** the sacred flame.
They do not shrink hereafter; **rather seek**
More converse, but with graver voices speak.

LIII.

One theme at last preferred **to** every other,
    Joying to talk of that mysterious land
Where each enshrines **the** image of a mother,
    Best **of** all watchers in the guardian band;
To highest, tenderest thought **is** freedom given
Amid this unembarrass'd air **of** Heaven.

LIV.

For when a hymn **has wing'd** itself away
    On Palestrina's full-resounding chords,
And at the trellis'd window **loiter** they,
    Deferring their goodnight with happy **words,**
Almost they know, without a throb of **fear,**
Of spirits in the twilight standing near.

LV.

And day by day and week **by** week pass by,
    And Love still poised upon a trembling plume
Floats on the very verge of sovereignty,
    Where ev'n a look may call him to assume
The rich apparel and the shining throne,
And claim two loyal subjects for his own.

LVI.

Wondrous, that first, full, mutual look of love
    Coming ere either looker is aware;
Unbounded trust, a tenderness above
    All tenderness; mute music, speechless pray'r;
Life's mystery, reality, and might,
Soft-swimming in a single ray of light!

LVII.

O when shall fly this talismanic gleam,
    Which melts like lightning every prison-bar,
Which penetrates the mist with keener beam
    Than flows from sun or moon or any star?
Love waits; like vulgar pebble of the ground
Th' imperial gem lies willing to be found.

LVIII.

One evening, Gerald came before his hour,
    Distrustful of the oft-consulted clock;
And waits, with no companion, till his flow'r—
    Keeping the time as one of Flora's flock,
Whose shepherdess, the Sunset Star, doth fold
Each in its leaves—he may again behold.

LIX.

Nor thinks it long. Familiar all, and dear,
    A sanctity pervades the silent room.
Autumnal is the season of the year;
    A mystic softness and love-weighty gloom
Gather with twilight. In a dream he lays
His hand on the piano, dreaming plays.

LX.

Most faint and broken sounds at first are stealing
   Into the shadowy stillness; wild and slow
Imperfect cadences of captive feeling,
   Gathering its strength, and yet afraid to know
Its chance of freedom,—till on murmuring chords
Th' unguarded thought strays forth in passionate words

LXI.

Angel of Music! when our finest speech
   Is all too coarse to give the heart relief,
The inmost fountains lie within thy reach,
   Soother of every joy and every grief;
And to the stumbling words thou lendest wings
On which aloft th' enfranchised spirit springs.

LXII.

Much love may in not many words be told;
   And on the sudden love can speak the best.
These mystical melodious buds unfold,
   On every petal showing clear imprest
The name of *Love*. So Gerald sung and play'd
Unconscious of himself, in twilight shade.

LXIII.

He has not overheard (O might it be!)
   This stifled sobbing at the open door,
Where Milly stands arrested tremblingly
   By that which in an instant tells her more
Than all the dumb months mused of; tells it plain
To joy that cannot comprehend its gain.

LXIV.

One moment, and they shall be face to face,
   Free in the gift of this great confidence,
Wrapt in the throbbing calm of its embrace,
   No more to disunite their spirits thence.
The myrtle crown stoops close to either brow,—
But ah! what alien voice distracts them now?

LXV.

Her sister comes. And Milly turns away;
   Hurriedly bearing to some quiet spot
Her tears and her full heart, longing to lay
   On a dim pillow cheeks so moist and hot.
When midnight stars between her curtains gleam
Fair Milly sleeps, and dreams a happy dream.

LXVI.

O dream, poor child! beneath the midnight stars;
   O slumber through the kindling of the dawn;
The shadow's on its way; the storm that mars
   The lily even now is hurrying on.
All has been long fulfill'd; yet I could weep
At thought of thee so quietly asleep.

LXVII.

But Gerald, through the night serenely spread,
   Walks quickly home, intoxicate with bliss
Not named and not examined; overhead
   The clustering lights of worlds are full of this
New element; the soft wind's dusky wings
Grow warmer on his cheek, with whisperings

LXVIII.

And yet to-night he has not seen his Love.
  His Love—in that one word all comfort dwells;
Reaching from earth to those clear flames above,
  And making common food of miracles.
Kind pulsing Nature, touch of Deity,
Sure thou art full of love, which lovers see!

LXIX.

Most cruel Nature, so unmoved, so hard,
  The while thy children shake with joy or pain!
Thou wilt not forward Love, nor Death retard
  One finger-push, for mortal's dearest gain.
Our Gerald, through the night serenely spread,
Walks quickly home, and finds his father dead.

LXX.

Great awe must be when the last blow comes down,
  Though but the ending of a weary strife,
Though years on years weigh low the hoary crown,
  Or sickness tenant all the house of life;
Stupendous ever is the great event,
The frozen form most strangely different!

LXXI.

To Gerald follow'd many doleful days,
  Like wet clouds moving through a sullen sky.
A vast unlook'd-for change the mind dismays,
  And smites its world with instability;
Rocks appear quaking, towers and treasures vain,
Peace foolish, Joy disgusting, Hope insane.

LXXII.

For even Cloonamore, that image dear,
  Returns to Gerald's mind like its own ghost,
In melancholy garments, drench'd and sere,
  Its joy, its colour, and its welcome lost.
Wanting one token sure to lean upon,
(How almost gained !) his happy dream is gone.

LXXIII.

Distracted purposes, a homeless band,
  Throng in his meditation, now he flies
To rest his soul on Milly's cheek and hand,—
  Now he makes outcry on his fantasies
For busy cheats : the lesson not yet learn'd
How Life's true coast from vapour is discern'd.

LXXIV.

Ah me ! 'tis like the tolling of a bell
  To hear it—" Past is past, and gone is gone ; "
With looking back afar to see how well
  We could have 'scaped our losses, and have won
High fortune. Ever greatest turns on least,
Like Earth's own whirl to atom poles decreased.

LXXV.

For in the gloomiest hour a letter came,
  Shot arrow-like across the Western sea,
Praising the West; its message was the same
  As many a time ere now had languidly
Dropp'd at his feet, but this the rude gale bore
To heart,—Gerald will quit our Irish shore.

LXXVI.

And quit his Love whom he completely loves;
　Who loves him just as much? Nay, downcast yout
Nay, dear mild maiden!—Surely it behoves
　That somewhere in the day there should be ruth
For innocent blindness?—lead, oh, lead them now
One step, but one!—Their fates do not allow.

LXXVII.

The parting scene is brief and frosty dumb.
　The unlike sisters stand alike unmoved;
For Milly's soul is wilder'd, weak, and numb,
　That reft away which seem'd so dearly proved.
While thought and speech she struggles to recover
Her hand is prest—and he is gone for ever.

LXXVIII.

Time speeds: on an October afternoon
　Across the well-known view he looks his last;
The valley clothed with peace and fruitful boon,
　The chapel where such happy hours were pass'd,
With rainbow-colour'd foliage round its eaves,
And windows all a-glitter through the leaves.

LXXIX.

The cottage-smokes, the river;—gaze no more,
　Sad heart! although thou canst not, wouldst not sh
The vision future years will oft restore,
　Whereon the light of many a summer sun,
The stars of many a winter night shall be
Mingled in one strange sighing memory.

END OF PART I.

THE MUSIC-MASTER.

A LOVE STORY.

PART II.

I.

THE shadow Death o'er Time's broad dial creeps
    With never-halting pace from mark to mark,
Blotting the sunshine; as it coldly sweeps,
    Each living symbol melts into the dark,
And changes to the name of what it was;—
Shade-measured light, progression proved by loss.

II.

Blithe Spring expanding into Summer's cheer,
    Great Summer ripening into Autumn's glow,
The yellow Autumn and the wasted year,
    And hoary-headed Winter stooping slow
Under the dark arch up again to Spring,
Have five times compass'd their appointed ring.

III.

See once again our village; with its street
    Dozing in dusty sunshine. All around
Is silence; save, for slumber not unmeet,
    Some spinning-wheel's continuous whirring sound
From cottage door, where, stretch'd upon his side,
The moveless dog is basking, drowsy-eyed.

IV.

The hollyhocks that **rise** above a wall
  Sleep in the richness of their crusted blooms;
Up the hot glass the sluggish blue flies crawl;
  The heavy bee **is humming** into rooms
Through open window, like a **sturdy** rover,
Bringing with **him warm scents of thyme and** clove

V.

With herb and flow'r you smell the ripening fruit
  In cottage gardens, on **the sultry** air;
But every bird has vanish'd, hiding mute
  In eave and hedgerow; save that here and there
With twitter swift, the sole unrestful thing,
Shoots the dark lightning of a swallow's wing.

VI.

Yet in this hour **of** sunny peacefulness
  One is there whom its influence little **calms,**
One who now leans in agony to press
  His throbbing forehead **with** his throbbing palm
Now paces quickly up and down within
The narrow parlour of **the** village inn.

VII.

He thought he **could** have tranquilly beheld
  The scene again. He thought his faithful grief,
Spread level in the soul, could not have swell'd
  To find once more a passionate relief.
Three years, they now seem hours, have sigh'd th
    breath
Since when he heard the tidings of her death.

VIII.

Last evening in the latest dusk he came,
  A holy pilgrim from a distant land;
And objects of familiar face and name,
  As at the wave of a miraculous wand,
Rose round his steps; his bed-room window show'd
His small white birthplace just across the road.

IX.

Yet in that room he could not win repose;
  The image of the past perplex'd his mind;
Often he sigh'd and turn'd and sometimes rose
  To bathe his forehead in the cool night-wind,
And vaguely watch the curtain broad and gray
Lifting anew from the bright scene of day.

X.

When creeping sultry hours from noontide go,
  He rounds the hawthorn hedge's wellknown turn,
Melting in Midsummer its bloomy snow,
  And through the chapel gate. His heart forlorn
Draws strength and comfort from the pitying shrine
Whereat he bows with reverential sign.

XI.

Behind the chapel, down a sloping hill,
  Circling the ancient abbey's ivied walls
The graveyard sleeps. A little gurgling rill
  Pour'd through a corner of the ruin, falls
Into a dusky-water'd pond, and lags
With lazy eddies 'mid its yellow flags.

XII.

Across this pool, the hollow banks enfold
   An orchard, overrun with rankest grass,
Of gnarl'd and mossy apple-trees as old
   As th' oldest graves almost; and thither pass
The smooth-worn stepping-stones that give their aid
To many a labourer and milking-maid.

XIII.

And not unfrequently to rustic **bound**
   On a more solemn errand. When we see
A suppliant in such universal ground,
   Let all be reverence **and sympathy;**
Assured the life in every real pray'r
Is that which makes **our life of life to share.**

XIV.

But resting in the sunshine very lone
   Is each green hummock now, each wooden cross;
And save the rillet in its **cup of** stone
   That poppling falls, and whispers through the moss
Down to the quiet pool, **no** sound is near
To break the stillness **to Gerald's ear.**

XV.

The writhen elder spreads its creamy bloom;
   The thicket-tangling, tenderest briar-rose
Kisses to air its exquisite perfume
   In shy luxuriance; spiry **foxglove** glows
With elvish crimson;—**nor** all **vainly** greet
The eye which unobserved they seem to **meet.**

XVI.

Under the abbey wall he wends his way,
  Admitted through a portal arching deep,
To where no roof excludes the common day;
  Though some few tombstones in the shadows sleep
Of hoary fibres and a throng of leaves,
Which venerable ivy slowly weaves.

XVII.

First hither comes, in piety of heart,
  Over his mother's, father's grave to bend,
The faithful exile. Let us stand apart,
  While his sincere and humble pray'rs ascend,
As such devout aspirings do, we trust,
To Him who sow'd them in our breathing dust.

XVIII.

And veil our very thoughts lest they intrude
  (Oh, silent death! oh, living pain full sore!)
Where lies enwrapt in grassy solitude
  That gentle matron's grave, of Cloonamore;
And on the stone these added words are seen—
"Also, her daughter Milly, aged eighteen."

XIX.

Profound the voiceless aching of the breast,
  When weary life is like a gray dull eve
Emptied of colour, withering and waste
  Around the prostrate soul, too weak to grieve—
Stretch'd far below the tumult and strong cry
Of passion—its lamenting but a sigh.

XX.

Grief's mystery desire not to disperse,
   Nor wish the secret of the world outspoken;
'Tis not a toy, this vital Universe,
   That thus its inner caskets may be broken.
Sorrow and pain, as well as hope and love,
Stretch out of view into the heavens above.

XXI.

Yet, oh! the cruel coldness of the grave,
   The keen remembrance of the happy past,
The thoughts which are at once tyrant and slave,
   The sudden sense that drives the soul aghast,
The drowning horror, and the speechless strife,
That fain would sink to death or rise to life!

XXII.

As Gerald lifted up his pallid face,
   He grew aware that he was not alone.
Amid the silence of the sacred place
   Another form was stooping o'er the stone;
A grayhair'd woman's. When she met his eyes
She shriek'd aloud in her extreme surprise.

XXIII.

"The Holy Mother keep us day and night!
   And who is this?—Oh, Master Gerald, dear,
I little thought to ever see this sight!
   Warm to the King above I offer here
My praises for the answer he has sent
To all my pray'rs; for now I'll die content!"

XXIV.

Then, as if talking to herself, she said,
   "I nursed her when she was a little child.
I smooth'd the pillow of her dying bed.
   And just the way that she had often smiled
When sleeping in her cradle—that same look
Was on her face with the last kiss I took."

XXV.

" 'Twas in the days of March," she said again.
   " And so it is the sweetest blossom dies,
The wrinkled leaf hangs on, though falling fain.
   I thought your hand would close my poor old eyes,
And not that I'd be sitting in the sun
Beside your grave,—the Lord's good will be done !"

XXVI.

Thus incoherently the woman spoke,
   With many interjections full of woe ;
And wrapping herself up within her cloak
   Began to rock her body to and fro ;
And moaning softly, seem'd to lose all sense
Of outward life in memories so intense.

XXVII.

Till Gerald burst his silence and exclaim'd,
   With the most poignant earnestness of tone,
" O nurse, I loved her !—though I never named
   The name of love to her, or any one.
'Tis to her grave here——" He could say no more,
But these few words a load of meaning bore.

XXVIII.

Beside the tombstone mute they both remain'd.
   At last the woman rose, and coming near,
Said with a tender voice that had regain'd
   A tremulous calm, "Then you must surely hear
The whole from first to last, *cushla-ma-chree;*
For God has brought together you and me."

XXIX.

And there she told him all the moving tale,
   Broken with many tears and sobs and sighs;
How gentle Milly's health began to fail;
   How a sad sweetness grew within her eyes,
And trembled on her mouth, so kind and meek,
And flush'd across her pale and patient cheek.

XXX.

And how about this time her sister Ann
   "Entered Religion,"[1] and her father's thought
Refused in Milly's face or voice to scan,
   Or once so lively step, the change that wrought;
Until a sad conviction flew at last,
And with a barb into his bosom pass'd.

XXXI.

Then, with most anxious haste, her dear old nurse
   Was sent for to become her nurse again;

---

[1] Took conventual vows.

But still the pretty one grew worse and worse.
  For with a gradual lapsing, free of pain,
And slow removes, that fond eyes would not see,
Crept on the hopeful, hopeless malady.

XXXII.

Spring came, and brought no gift of life to her,
  Of all it lavish'd in the fields and woods.
Yet she was cheer'd when birds began to stir
  About the shrubbery, and the pale gold buds
Burst on the willows, and with hearty toil
The ploughing teams upturn'd the sluggish soil.

XXXIII.

" 'Twas on a cold March evening, well I mind,"
  The nurse went on, " we sat and watch'd together
The long gray sky; and then the sun behind
  The clouds shone down, though not like summer weather,
On the hills far away. I can't tell why,
But of a sudden I began to cry.

XXXIV.

" I dried my tears before I turn'd to her,
  But then I saw that her eyes too were wet,
And pale her face, and calm without a stir;
  Whilst on the lighted hills her look was set,
Where strange beyond the cold dark fields they lay,
As if her thoughts, too, journey'd far away.

XXXV.

"After a while she ask'd me to unlock
  A drawer, and bring a little parcel out.
I knew it was of it she wish'd to talk,
  But long she held it in her hand in doubt;
And whilst she strove, there came a blush and spread
Her face and neck with a too passing red.

XXXVI.

"At length she put her other hand in mine;
  'Dear nurse,' she said, 'I'm sure I need not ask
Your promise to fulfil what I design
  To make my last request, and your last task.
You knew young Master Gerald' (here her speech
Grew plain) 'that used to come here once to teach?

XXXVII.

"I said I knew you well; and she went on,—
  'Then listen: if you ever see him more,
And he should speak of days are past and gone,
  And of his scholars and his friends before—
Should ask you questions—knowing what you've been
To me,—Oh! could I tell you what I mean!'

XXXVIII.

"But, sir, I understood her meaning well;
  Not from her words so much as from her eyes.
I saw it all; my heart began to swell,
  I took her in my arms with many sighs
And murmurs, and she lean'd upon my neck
Till we both cried our fill without a check.

XXXIX.

"She saw I knew her mind, and bade me give
    Into your hand, if things should so befall,
The parcel;—else, as long as I should live,
    It was to be a secret kept from all,
And say you never wrote, never return'd,
When my last hour drew near, was to be burn'd.

XL.

" I promised to observe her wishes duly;
    But said I hoped in God that she would still
Live many years beyond myself. And truly
    While she was speaking, like a miracle
Her countenance lost every sickly trace.
Ah, dear! 'twas setting light was in her face.

XLI.

" She told me she was tired, and went to bed,
    And I sat watching by her until dark,
And then I lit her lamp, and round her head
    Let down the curtains. 'Twas my glad remark
How softly she was breathing, and my mind
Was full of hope and comfort,—but we're blind!

XLII.

" The night wore on, and I had fall'n asleep,
    When about three o'clock I heard a noise
And sprang up quickly. In the silence deep
    Was some one praying with a calm weak voice;
Her own voice, though not sounding just the same;
And in the pray'r I surely heard *your* name.

XLIII.

"Sweet Heaven! we scarce had time to fetch the priest
   How sadly through the shutters of that room
Crept in the blessed daylight from the east
   To us that sat there weeping in the gloom;
And touch'd the close-shut eyes and peaceful brow,
But brought no fear of her being restless now.

XLIV.

"The wake was quiet. Noiseless went the hours
   Where she was lying stretch'd so still and white;
And near the bed, a glass with some Spring flowers
   From her own little garden. Day and night
I watch'd, until they took my lamb away,
The child here by the mother's side to lay.

XLV.

"The holy angels make your bed, my dear!
   But little call have we to pray for you:
Pray you for him that's left behind you here,
   To have his heart consoled with heavenly dew!
And pray too for your poor old nurse, *asthore;*
Your own true mother scarce could love you more!"

XLVI.

Slow were their feet amongst the many graves,
   Over the stile and up the chapel-walk,
Where stood the poplars with their timid leaves
   Hung motionless on every slender stalk.
The air in one hot calm appear'd to lie,
And thunder mutter'd in the heavy sky.

XLVII.

Along the street was heard the laughing sound
  Of boys at play, who knew no thought of death ;
Deliberate-stepping cows, to milking bound,
  Lifted their heads and low'd with fragrant breath ;
The women knitting at their thresholds cast
A look upon our stranger as he pass'd.

XLVIII.

Scarce had the mourners time a roof to gain,
  When, with electric glare and thunder-crash,
Heavy and straight and fierce came down the rain,
  Soaking the white road with its sudden plash,
Driving all folk within-doors at a race,
And making every kennel gush apace.

XLIX.

The storm withdrew as quickly as it came,
  And through the broken clouds a brilliant ray
Glow'd o'er the dripping earth in yellow flame,
  And flush'd the village panes with parting day.
Sudden and full that swimming lustre shone
Into the room where Gerald sat alone.

L.

The door is lock'd, and on the table lies
  The open parcel. Long he wanted strength
To trust its secrets to his feverish eyes ;
  But now the message is convey'd at length ;—
A note ; a case ; and folded with them there
One finest ringlet of brown-auburn hair.

LI.

The case holds Milly's portrait—her reflection:
　Lips lightly parted, as about to speak;
The frank broad brow, young eyes of grave affection,
　Even the tender shadow on the cheek:
Swift image of a moment snatch'd from Time,
Fix'd by a sunbeam in eternal prime.

LII.

The note ran thus, " Dear Gerald, near my death,
　I feel that like a Spirit's words are these,
In which I say, that I have perfect faith
　In your true love for me,—as God, who sees
The secrets of all hearts, can see in mine
That fondest truth which sends this feeble sign.

LIII.

" I do not think that he will take away,
　Even in Heaven, this precious earthly love;
Surely he sends its pure and blissful ray
　Down as a message from the world above.
Perhaps it is the full light drawing near
Which makes the doubting Past at length grow clear.

LIV.

"We might have been so happy!—But His will
　Said no, who orders all things for the best.
O may his power into your soul instil
　A peace like this of which I am possess'd!
And may he bless you, love, for evermore,
And guide you safely to his Heavenly shore!"

LV.

Hard sits the downy pillow to a head
  Aching with memories: and Gerald sought
The mournful paths where happy hours had fled,—
  Pacing through silent labyrinths of thought.
Yet sometimes, in his loneliness of grief,
The richness of the loss came like relief.

LVI.

Minutely he recall'd, with tender pride,
  How one day—which is gone for evermore—
Among his bunch of wild flowers left aside,
  He found a dark carnation, seen before
In Milly's girdle,—but alas, too dull
To read its crimson cypher in the full!

LVII.

She smiled, the centre of a summer's eve:
  She sung, with all her countenance a-glow,
In her own room, and he could half believe
  The voice did far-off in the darkness flow:
He saw her stretch'd in a most silent place,
With the calm light of prayer upon her face.

LVIII.

All this night long the water-drops he heard
  Vary their talk of chiming syllables,
Dripping into the butt; and in the yard
  The ducks gabbling at daylight; till the spells
Of misty sense recall'd a childish illness
When the same noises broke the watching stillness.

LIX.

Wellnigh he hoped that he had sadly dream'd,
  And all the interval was but a shade.
But now the slow dawn through his window gleam'd
  And whilst in dear oblivion he was laid,
And Morning rose, parting the vapours dim,
A happy heavenly vision came to him.

LX.

Kind boons of comfort may in dream descend,
  Nor wholly vanish in the broad daylight.
—When this our little story hath an end,
  That flickers like a dream in woof of night,
Its slender memory may perchance be wrought
Among the tougher threads of waking thought?

LXI.

Thus Gerald came and went. Till far away,
  His coming and his errand were not told.
And years had left behind that sunny day,
  Ere some one from the New World to the Old
Brought news of him, in a great Southern town,
Assiduous there, but seeking no renown.

LXII.

After another silent interval,
  The little daily lottery of the post
Gave me a prize; from one who at the call
  Of "westward ho!" had left our fair green coast,
With comrades eager as himself to press
Into the rough unharrow'd wilderness.

LXIII.

"Through these old forests (thus he wrote) we came
   One sundown to a clearing. Western light
Burn'd in the pine-tops with a fading flame
   Over untrodden regions, and dusk night
Out of the solemn woods appear'd to rise
To some strange music, full of quivering sighs.

LXIV.

"Such must have been the atmosphere, we thought,
   The visionary light of ancient years,
When Red Man east or west encounter'd nought
   Save bear and squirrel, with their wild compeers.
But other life was now; and soon we found
The little citadel of this new ground.

LXV.

"The neat log-cabin from its wall of pines
   Look'd out upon a space of corn and grass
Yet thick with stumps; 'twas eaved with running vines,
   As though among the vanquish'd woods to pass
For something native. Drawing to its door,
We question'd of the mystic sounds no more.

LXVI.

"They blended with the twilight and the trees,
   At hand, around, above, and far away,
That first it was a voice as of the breeze
   Hymning its vespers in the forest gray;
But now we heard not airy strains alone,
But human feeling throb in every tone.

s

LXVII.

"A swelling agony of tearful strife
   Being wearied out and hush'd,—from the profound
Arose a music deep as love or life,
   That spread into a placid lake of sound,
And took the infinite into its breast,
With Earth and Heaven in one embrace at rest;

LXVIII.

"And then the flute-notes fail'd. Approaching slow
   Whom found we seated in the threshold shade?
Gerald,—our Music-Master long ago
   In poor old Ireland; much inquiry made
Along our track for him had proved in vain;
And here at once we grasp'd his hand again!

LXIX.

"And he received us with the warmth of heart
   Our brothers lose not under any sky.
But what was strange, he did not stare or start
   As if astonish'd, when, so suddenly,
Long-miss'd familiar faces from the wood
Emerged like ghosts, and at his elbow stood.

LXX.

"'Twas like a man who joyfully was greeting
   (So thought I) some not unexpected friends.
And yet he had not known our chance of meeting
   More than had we: but soon he made amends
For lack of wonder, by the dextrous zeal
That put before us no unwelcome meal.

LXXI.

" We gave him all our news, and in return
    He told us how he lived,—a lonely life!
Miles from a neighbour sow'd and reap'd his corn,
    And hardy grew. One spoke about a wife
To cheer him in that solitary wild,
But Gerald only shook his head and smiled.

LXXII.

" Next dawn, when each one of our little band
    Had on a mighty Walnut carved his name,—
Henceforth a sacred tree, he said, to stand
    'Mid his enlarging bounds,—the moment came
For farewell words. But long, behind our backs,
We heard the echoes of his swinging axe."

PRINCE BRIGHTKIN.

Scene: A Forest in Fairyland.

DAWN.

First Fairy. FAIRIES and Elves!
　　Gone is the night,
Shadows grow thin,
　　Branches are stirr'd;
Rouse up yourselves,
　　Sing to the light,
Fairies, begin,—
　　There goes a bird!

Second. For dreams are now fading,
Old thoughts **in new** morning;
Dull spectres and goblins
　　To dungeon must fly.
The starry night chang**eth**,
Its low stars are setting,
Its lofty stars dwindle
　　And hide **in the sky.**

First.　　Fairies, awake!
　　　　Light on the hills!
Blossom and grass
　　Tremble with dew;
Gambols the snake,
　　Merry bird shrills,
Honey-bees pass,
　　Morning is **new.**

Second. Pure joy of the cloudlets,
All rippled in crimson!
Afar over world's edge
  The night-fear is roll'd;
O look how the Great One
Uplifts himself kingly;
At once the wide morning
  Is flooded with gold!

First. Fairies, arouse!
  Mix with your song
Harplet and pipe,
  Thrilling and clear.
Swarm on the boughs!
  Chant in a throng!
Morning is ripe,
  Waiting to hear.

Second. The merle and the skylark
Will hush for our chorus,
Quick wavelets of music,
  Begin them anon!
Good-luck comes to all things
That hear us and hearken,—
Our myriads of voices
  Commingling in one.

General **Chorus.** Golden, golden
  Light unfolding,
Busily, merrily, work and play,
  In flowery meadows,

  And forest-shadows,
All the length of a summer day!
All the length of a summer day!

  Sprightly, lightly,
  Sing we rightly!
Moments brightly hurry away!
  Fruit-tree blossoms,
  And roses' bosoms,—
Clear blue sky of a summer day!
Dear blue sky of a summer day!

  Springlets, brooklets,
  Greeny nooklets,
Hill and valley, and salt-sea spray!
  Comrade rovers,
  Fairy lovers,—
All the length of a summer day!
All the livelong summer day!

FORENOON.

Enter two Fairies (ROSLING *and* Another) *separately*.

First.   Greeting, brother!

Second.   Greet thee well!
Hast thou any news to tell?
How goes sunshine?

First.   Flowers of noon
All their eyes will open soon,
While ours are closing. What hast done
Since the rising of the sun?

Second.   Four wild snails I've taught their paces,
　　　　　Pick'd the best one for the races.
　　　　　Thou?

First.   　　Where luscious dewdrops lurk,
　　　　　I with fifty went to work,
　　　　　Catching delicious wine that wets
　　　　　The warm blue heart of violets;
　　　　　Last moon it was hawthorn-flower,
　　　　　Next moon 'twill be virgin's bower,
　　　　　Moon by moon, the varied rose,—
　　　　　To seal in flasks for winter mirth,
　　　　　When frost and darkness wrap the earth.
　　　　　Which wine delights you, fay?

Second.   　　　　　　　　All those;
　　　　　But none is like the Wine of Rose.
　　　　　　　With Wine of Rose,
　　　　　　　In midst of snows
　　　　　The sunny season flows and glows!

First.   Elf, thou lovest best, I think,
　　　　　The time to sit in a cave and drink.

Second.   Is 't not well to have good reason,
　　　　　Thus, for loving every season?
　　　　　　　Whiterose-wine
　　　　　　　Is pure and fine,
　　　　　But Redrose-dew, dear tipple of mine!
　　　　　　　The red flow'rs bud

In our summery blood,
And the nightingale sings in our brain, like
    a wood!

First.   Some who came a-gathering dew,
Tasting, sipping, fresh and new,
Tumbled down, an idle crew,
And there among the grass they lie,
Under a toadstool; any fly
May nip their foolish noses!

Second.   Soon
We shall hear the Call of Noon.

First.   They cannot stir to any tune.
No evening feast for them, be sure,
But far-off sentry on the moor.
Whence that sound of music?—hist!

Second.   Klingoling, chief lutanist,
A hundred song-birds in a ring
Is teaching all this morn to sing
Together featly, so to fill
The wedding-music,—loud and shrill,
Soft and sweet, and high and low,
Singled, mingled. He doth know
The art to make a hundred heard
Like one great surprising bird.

First.   Here comes Rosling! He'll report
All the doings of the court.

Enter a Third Fairy.

Greeting, brothers!

First. Greet thee well!
Hast thou any news to tell?
Our Princess dear, what shadow lies
Drooping on her blissful eyes?
Her suitors plague her?—is it so?

Third. So in truth it is. But, lo!
Who comes our way? Fairy, whence?
Thou 'rt a stranger.

Enter a Fourth Fairy.

No offence,
I trust, altho' my cap is blue,
While yours are green as any leaf.
Courteous fays! no spy or thief
Is here, but one who longs to view
Your famous Forest; chiefly there
Your Princess fair, the praised in song
Wheresoever fairies throng.
Oft you see her?

Third. Every day.

Fourth. And is she lovely as they say?

Third. Thou hast not seen her? Dost thou think
Blue and golden, white and pink,
Could paint the magic of her face?
All common beauty's highest place
Being under hers how far!—

Fourth. How far?

Third. A glowworm to the evening-star.

First. Scarce Klingoling could say so well!
'Tis true : so much she doth excel.
Come, fairy, to our feast to-night,
Two hours from sunset ; then you may
See the Forest-Realm's Delight.

Fourth. But were it not presumptuous?

First. Nay,
Thou art, I ween, a gentle fay,
And sure of welcome.

Fourth. It is said
Her Highness shortly means to wed?

Third. Next full moon, by fairy law,
She must marry, no escape,
Were it marsh-sprite, kobold, shape
Creeping from earth-hole with horn and claw

Fourth. And hath she now a suitor?

Third. Three ;
Bloatling, Rudling, Loftling ; she
Loathes them all impartially.
The first is ugly, fat, and rich,
Grandson of a miser-witch ;
He sends her bossy peonies,
Fat as himself, to please her eyes,

And double-poppies, mock flow'rs made
In clumsy gold, for brag display'd;
Ten of the broadest-shoulder'd elves
To carry one must strain themselves.

First.   Aye! so I've seen them.

Second.   This is more
Than I ever heard before.

Third.   Field-marshal Rudling, soldier fay,
His beard a broom to sweep away
Opposition, with his frown
Biddeth common fairies " Down!
" Down on your knees!" and then his smile,
Our lovely Lady's heart to wile—
Soft as a rat-trap! and his voice—
Angry jay makes no such noise
When bold marauders threat (as you,
Little Jinkling, sometimes do)
Her freckled eggs.

Fourth.   And Loftling?

Third.   True.
Prince Loftling's chin, so grand is he,
Is where another's nose would be;
His high backbone the wrong way bends
With nobleness. He condescends
To come in state to our poor wood;
And then 'tis always understood

> We silence every prattling bird,
> Nor must one grasshopper be heard;
> Which tasks our people; she, meanwhile,
> Our Lady, half-dead with his vile
> Ceremonial and precision,—
> " Madam, with your august permission,
> " I have the honour to remark—
> " Ah hum! ah haw!" from dawn to dark.

Fourth. He will not win her?

Third. No, no, no!
> Dreary the wood if that were so,
> Good stranger. But enough, I ween,
> Of gossip now.

Fourth. Kind Caps o' Green,
> I thank ye for your courtesies!
> Brightkin's my name, my country lies
> Round that blue peak your scout espies
> From loftiest fir-tree on the skies
> Of sunset. So I take my leave
> Till the drawing-on of eve.

First. They call me Rosling, gentle fay.
> Adieu! forget not; here I'll stay
> To meet thee and to show the way.

All. Adieu! adieu! till close of day.

THE NOON-CALL.

Hear the call!
Fays, be still!
Noon is deep
On vale and hill.
Stir no sound
The Forest round!
Let all things hush
That fly or creep,—
Tree and bush,
Air and ground!
Hear the call!
Silence keep!
One and all
Hush, and sleep!

NEAR SUNSET.

Two Fairies: ROSLING *and* JINKLING.

Ros.   Little Jinkling! friend of mine!
Where dost lurk when fairies dine?
All the banquet round and round
Searching, thee I never found.
Comest thou late? The feast is done;
Slowly sinks the mighty sun.

Jink.   Nay, fay! I was far away.
Over the tree-tops did I soar

  Twenty leagues and twenty more.
  Swift and high goes the dragon-fly,
   And **steady the** death's-head moth,
  But the little bird with his beak awry
   Is a better saddle than both!
  The lovely Lady of Elfin-Mere,
  I had a message for her ear.

Ros. Of state?

Jink.   Of state: of import great,
  I must not even to thee relate.

Ros. And is she fair?

Jink.   Thrice-fair **is she:**
  The pearly moon less delicately
  Comes **shining on,** than when **this Lady**
  From her water-palace shady
  Floats across the lucent lake,
  And all her starry lilies make
  Obeisance; every water-sprite
  Gazing after with delight,
  Only wishing he might dare
  Just to touch her streaming hair.
  Meanwhile, crowds of fairies glide
  Over, under, the crystal tide,
  Some **on** swimming-birds astride,
  Some with merry fishes **at play,**
  Darting round her rippling way.

Ros.   There was your banquet?

Jink.   There indeed,
          Among the lily and the reed.
          Wavy music, as we feasted,
          Floating round us while we floated,
          Soothed our pleasure and increased it;
          Mirth and jest more gaily glancing
          Than the water-diamonds dancing
          Down the lake where sunshine smote it.
          Bright and gay!—might not stay!—
          White the hand I kiss'd, O fay,
          Leap'd on my bird, and sped away.
          Hast any news to tell me?

Ros.   Much!
          Never didst thou hear of such.

Jink.   A fight with spiders?—hornets?—perils
          Teasing owls, or chasing squirrels?
          Or some little elf, poor soul,
          Lost in a winding rabbit-hole?
          Are the royal trees in danger?

Ros.   Dost thou mind the Blue-cap Stranger,
          Brightkin by his name, that we
          Met ere noontide lullaby?

Jink.   Came he to your Feast?

Ros.   My friend,
Ask no more questions, but attend!
To the Feast he came with me,
The chamberlain most courteously
Placing us nigh the upper end.
Her Highness bow'd, and Brightkin gazed
On her face like one amazed,
While the Princess's tender eyes
Rested with a sweet surprise
Upon the stranger-fairy: round
When cates and wines, and Klingoling
With five new birds began to sing.
Then came a page on errand bound
To ask the stranger's name and realm:
" Brightkin, of the Purple Helm,
" From the Blue Mountain, fairy knight,
" Flown thence to view the Forest,—might
" It please her Highness." It did please.
So by-and-by we sat at ease
In shadowy bow'r, a favour'd ring,
Now talking, now with Klingoling
Join'd in a waft of harmony;
And evermore there seem'd to be
'Twixt Brightkin and our Princess dear
A concord, more than string with string
And voice with voice rejoice one's ear.
At last *he* took the lute and sung,
   With modest grace and skilfully,
For tipt with honey seem'd his tongue;
   At first a murmuring melody,

    Like the far song of falling rills
    Amid the foldings of the hills,
    And ever nearer as it flew,
    Shaping its figure, like a bird,
    Till into Love's own form it grew
    In every lovely note and word.
    So sweet a song we never heard!
    When, think what came?

Jink.   I cannot think.

Ros.   A trumpet-blast that made us wink!
    A hailstorm upon basking flowers!
    Quick, sharp!—we started to our feet,
    All save her Highness, mild and sweet,
    Who said, "See who invades our bowers."

Jink.   Who was it, Rosling? quickly say!

Ros.   The King of the Blue Mountains, fay,
    Seeking audience, without delay.
    Fierce and frowning his look at first,
    Like that uncivil trumpet-burst;
    But all his blackness alter'd soon,
    Like clouds that melt upon the moon,
    Before the gentle dignity
    Of Her, Titania's child, whom we
    Obey and love.

Jink.   Blest may she be!
    But wherefore came the haughty King?

Ros.   Hear briefly an unusual thing.
His only son, the prince and heir,
Kept with too strict and jealous care
Within the mountain boundaries,
To-day o'erleaps them all, and flies,
No elf knows whither: flies to-day—
The Lord of Gnomes being on his way,
Bringing to that mountain court
His gem-clad heiress. Here was sport!
Then couriers told the angry king
They saw the prince on gray-dove's wing
Threading our forest; and again,
That he had join'd our Lady's train.
—" Madam! is't so?" "If this be so,
" Great sir, I nothing know." When lo!
Brightkin outspringing kneels. " My son!"
Exclaims the king—" Ho! seize and bind hi
But swift her Highness—" Stay! let none
" Move hand or foot! Great King, you find
" Here in the Forest-Realm, my rule
" Whereof no fairy power may school,
" Saving imperial Oberon.
" Free came he hither, free shall go.
" I nothing knew that this was so."
Then says the Prince, " If you command,
" I leave you, Pride of Fairyland,
" Else never!" Briefly now to tell,
As briefly all these things befell,
'Twas clear as new-born star they loved;
The Mountain-King their love approved;
And all were happy.

Jink.   Where are they,
The King and Prince, now?

Ros.   Flown away
On the sunset's latest ray.
To-morrow they will come again,
With a countless noble train;
And next full moon—the Wedding-Feast!

Jink.   O joy! the greatest and the least
Will join the revelry, and bring
A marriage-gift of some fine thing.
I know a present she will prize—
A team of spot-wing'd butterflies,
Right in flight, or else with ease
Winding through the tops of trees,
Or soaring in the summer sky.

Ros.   Well done, Jinkling!—now goodbye;
Sleepy as a field-mouse I,
When paws and snout coil'd he doth lie.

Jink.   Hark to Klingoling's lute-playing!
On the poplar-spire a-swaying
Gently to the crescent moon.

Ros.   I cannot stay to hear the tune.

Jink.   I linger in the drowsy light.

Ros.   And so, goodnight!

Jink.   And so, goodnight!

AFTER SUNSET.

Klingoling and a Faint Chorus.

Moon soon sets now :
Elves cradled on the bough.
Day's fays drop asleep :
Dreams through the forest **creep.**

Chorus. **When** broadens the moonlight, we frolic an
jest ;
When darkles the forest, we sink into rest.

Shine, fine star above !
Love's come, happy love !
Haste, happy wedding-night,
Full moon, round and bright !

Chorus. **And not till her** circle is low in the west
We 'll cease from our dancing, or couch t
to rest !

Lute, mute fall **thy strings** !
Hush, every voice that sings !
Low, slow, sleepy song,
Fade forest-aisles along !

Chorus. **Of all** thy sweet music a love-song is best !—
Thou hushest—we're silent—we sink int
rest.

SOUTHWELL PARK.

I.—FROM THE HIGHWAY.

"FRIEND Edward, from this turn remark
    A vista of the Bridegroom's Park,
Fair Southwell, shut while you were here
By selfish Cupid, who allows
A sunny glimpse through beechen boughs
Of dells of grass with fallow deer,
And one white corner of the house
Built for the young Heir's wedding-day,
The dull old walls being swept away.
Wide and low, its eaves are laid
Over a slender colonnade,
Partly hiding, partly seen,
Amid redundant veils of green,
Which garland pillars into bowers,
And top them with a frieze of flowers;
The slight fence of a crystal door
(Like air enslaved by magic lore)
Or window reaching to the floor,
Divides the richly furnish'd rooms
From terraces of emerald sward,
Vases full of scarlet blooms,
And little gates of rose, to guard
The sidelong steps of easy flight;
Or, with a touch, they all unite.
All's perfect for a Bride's delight,
And She a worthy queen of all;

Gold-hair'd (I've seen her), slim and tall;
With—O a true celestial face
Of tender gravity and grace,
And gentle eyes that look you through,
Eyes of softly solemn blue.

Serene the wealthy mortal's fate,
Whose last wild-oats is duly sown!
Observe his Paradise's gate,
With two heraldic brutes in stone
For sentries. Did the coppice move?
A straggling deer perhaps. By Jove!
A woman brushing through: she's gone.
Now what the deuce can bring her there?
Jog, lad: it's none of our affair.
  Well—you're to voyage, and I'm to stay.
Will Lucy kiss you, some other day,
When you carry your nuggets back this way?
You must not grow so rich and wise
That friends shall fail to recognize
The schoolboy-twinkle in your eyes.
Each his own track. I'll mind my farm,
And keep the old folk's chimney warm.
But however we strive, and chance to thrive,
We shall scarcely overtake this Youth,
Who has all to his wish, and seems in truth
The very luckiest man alive."

II.—BY THE POND.

" These walls of green, my Emmeline,
A labyrinth of shade and sheen,
Bar out the world a thousand miles,
Helping the pathway's winding wiles
To pose you to the end.   Now think,
What thanks might one deserve for this—
Which lately was a swamp, and is
An elfin lake, its curving brink
Embost with rhododendron bloom,
Azaleas, lilies, jewelries,
(Ruby and amethyst grow like these
Under our feet) on fire to dress,
Round every little glassy bay,
The sloping turf with gorgeousness?
As right, we look our best to-day ;
No petal dropt, no speck of gloom.

   Emmeline, this faery lake
Rose to its margins for your sake ;
As yet without a name, it sues
Your best invention ; think and choose.
Its flood is gather'd on the fells,
(Whose foldings you and I shall trace)
Hid in many a hollow place ;
But through Himalayan dells,
Where the silvery pinnacles
Hanging faint in furthest heaven
Catch the flames of morn and even,
Round their lowest rampart swells

The surge of rhododendron flow'rs,
Indian ancestry of ours:
And the tropic woods luxuriantly
By Oronooko's river-sea
Nurtured the germs of this and this:
And there's a blossom first was seen
In a dragon-vase of white and green
By the sweetheart of a mandarin,
Winking her little eyes for bliss.
   Look, how these merry insects go
In rippling meshes to and fro,
Waltzing over the liquid glass,
Dropping their shadows to cross and travel,
Like ghosts, on the pavement of sunny gravel.
Maybe to music, whose thrills outpass
Our finest ear,—yes, even yours,
Whom the mystery of sound allures
From star to star. In this gulf beyond,
Silent people of the pond
Slip from noonday glare, to win
Their crystal twilights far within.
See the creatures glance and hide,
Turn, and waver, and glimmer, and glide,
Jerk away, ascend, and poise,
Come and vanish without noise,
Mope, with mouth of drowsy drinking,
Waving fins and eyes unwinking,
Flirt a tail, and shoot below.
How little of their life we know!
Or these birds' life that twittering dart

To the shrubbery's woven heart.
Which is happier, bird or fish?
Have they memory, hope, and wish?
Various temper? perverse will—
That secret source of boundless ill?
Why should not human creatures run
A careless course through shadow and sun?
Ah, Love, that may never be!
We are of a different birth,
Of deeper sphere than the fishes' home,
Higher than bird's wings may roam,
Greater than ocean, air, and earth.

 The Summer's youth is now at prime.
Swiftly a season whirls away.
Two days past, the bladed corn
Whisper'd nothing of harvest-time;
Already a tinge of brown is born
On the barley-spears that lightly sway;
The plumes of purple-seeded grass,
Bowing and bending as you pass,
Our mowers at the break of day
Shall sweep them into swaths of hay.
So the season whirls away.
And every aspect we must learn,
Southwell's every mood discern;
All sides, over the country speed,
'She upon her milk-white steed,
And he upon his gray,' to roam
Gladly, turn more gladly home;
Plan, improve, and see our tenants;

Visit neighbours, for pleasure or penance ;
Excellent people some, no doubt,
And the rest will do to talk about.
June, July, and August : **next**
September comes ; and here we stand
To watch those swallows, some clear **day,**
With a birdish trouble, half perplex'd,
Bidding adieu in their tribe's old way,
Though the sunbeam coaxes them **yet to stay** ;
Swinging through the populous **air,**
Dipping, every bird, in play,
To kiss its flying image there.
And when Autumn's wealthy heavy hand
Paints with brown gold the beechen leaves,
And the wind comes cool, and the latest sheaves,
Quivers fill'd with bounty, rest
On stubble-slope,—then *we* shall say
Adieu for a time, our fading bow'rs,
Pictures within and out-of-doors,
And all the petted greenhouse flow'rs.
But, though your harp remains behind,
To keep the piano company,
Your light-strung Sprite of Serenades
Shall watch with us how daylight fades
Where sea and air enhance their dyes
A thousand-fold for lovers' eyes.
And we shall fancy on far-off coast
The chill pavilions of the frost,
And landscapes in a snow-wreath lost.
—You, the well-fended nun-like child,

I, the bold youth, left loose and wild,
Join'd together for evermore,
To wander at will by sea and shore,—
Strange and very strange it seems!
More like the shifting world of dreams.

   Choose a path, my Emmeline,
Through this labyrinth of green,
As though 'twere life's perplexing scene.
To go in search of your missing book,
You careless girl? one other search?
Wood or garden, which do you say?
'Twere only toil in vain: for, look—
I found it, free of spot or smirch,
On a pillow of wood-sorrel sleeping
Under the Fox's Cliff to-day.
Not so much as your place is lost,
Given to this delicate warden's keeping,—
Jasmin, that deserves to stay
Enshrined there henceforth, never toss'd
Like other dying blooms away.

   Summer, autumn, winter,—yes,
And much will come that we cannot guess;
Every minute brings its chance.

   Bend we now a parting glance
Down through the peaceful purity,
The shadow and the mystery,
As old saints look into their grave.
Water-elves may peep at me;
Only my own wife's face I see,
Like sunny light within the wave,

Dearer to me than sunny light.
It rose, and look'd away my night;
Whose phantoms, of desire or dread,
Like fogs and shades and dreams are fled."

III.—THROUGH THE WOOD.

" A fire keeps burning in this breast.
The smoke ascending to my brain
Sometimes stupefies the pain.
Sometimes my senses drop, no doubt.
I do not always feel the pain:
But my head is a weary weary load.
   What place is this?—I sit at rest,
With grass and bushes round about;
No dust, no noise, no endless road,
No torturing light. Stay, let me think,
Is this the place where I knelt to drink,
And all my hair broke loose and fell
And floated in the cold clear well
Hung with rock-weeds? two children came
With pitchers, but they scream'd and ran;
The woman stared, the cursèd man
Laugh'd,—no, no, this is not the same.
I now remember. Dragging through
The thorny fence has torn my gown.
These boots are very nearly done.
What matter? so's my journey too.

   Nearly done . . . A quiet spot!
Flowers touch my hand. It's summer now.

What summer meant I had forgot;
Except that it was glaring hot
Through tedious days, and heavy hot
Through dreadful nights.

                    The drooping bough
Is elm; its shadow lies below.
Gathering flowers, we used to creep
Along the hedgerows, where the sun
Came through like this; then, every one,
Find out some arbour close and cool,
To weave them in our rushy caps,—
Primroses, bluebells, such a heap,
Stay now!—the girls are hid perhaps—
It may be all a dream—
                      You fool!
Was it for this you made your way
To Southwell Park by night and day?
—A million times I used to say
These two words, lest they might be lost:
After a while, turn where I would
I heard them. . . . This is his domain;
Each tree is his, each blade of grass
Under my feet. How dare I pass,
A tatter'd vagrant, half insane,
Scarce fit to slink by the roadside,
These lordly bounds, where, with his Bride—
I tell you, kneeling on this sod,
He is, before the face of God,
My husband!

I was innocent
The day I first set eyes on him,
Eyes that no tears had yet made dim,
Nor fever wild. The day he went,
(That day, O **God of Heaven**!) I found,
In the sick brain slow turning **round**,
Dreadful forebodings of my fate.
A week was not so long to wait:
Another pass'd,—and then a third.
My face grew thin—eyes fix'd—I heard
And started if a feather stirr'd.
Each night 'to-morrow!' heard **me say,**
Each morning 'he will come to-day.'
Who taps upon the chamber door?—
A letter—he will come no more.
Then stupor. Then **a** horrid strife
Trampling my brain and soul and life,—
Hunting me out as with a knife
From home—from home—

       And I was young,
And happy. May his heart be **wrung**
As mine is! learn that **even** I
Was something, and **at least can die**
Of such a wound. **In** any case
He'll see the death that's in my face.
To die is still within the power
Of girls with neither rank nor dower.

 This is Southwell. **I am here.**
The house lay that side as **one came.**

How sick and deadly tired I am!
Time has been lost: O this new fear,
That I may fall and never rise!
Clouds come and go within my eyes.
I'm hot and cold, my limbs all slack,
My swollen feet the same as dead;
A weight like lead draws down my head,
The boughs and brambles pull me back.
Stay: the wood opens to the hill.
A moment now. The house is near.
But one may view it closer still
From these thick laurels on the right,
. . . What is this? Who come in sight?
He, with his Bride. It sends new might
Through all my feeble body. Hush!
Which way? which way? which way? that bush
Hides them—they're coming—do they pause?
He points, almost to me!—he draws
Her tow'rds him, and I know the smile
That's on his face—O heart of guile!
No, 'twas the selfish gaiety
And arrogance of wealth. I see
Your Bride is tall, and graceful too.
That arch of leaves invites you through.
I follow. Why should I be loth
To hurt her? . . . Ha! I'll find them both.
Six words suffice to make her know.
Both, both shall hear—it must be so!"

IV.—MOSSGROWN.

"Seven years gone, and we together
Ramble as before, old Ned!
Not a brown curl on your head
Soil'd with touch of time or weather.
Yet no wonder if you fear'd,
With that broad chest and bushy beard,
Lucy might scarce remember you.
My letters, had they painted true
The child grown woman?
       Here's our way.
Autumn is in its last decay;
The hills have misty solitude
And silence; dead leaves drop in the wood;
And free in Southwell Park we stray,
Where only the too-much freedom baulks.
These half-obliterated walks,
The tangling grass, the shrubberies choked
With briars, the runnel which has soak'd
Its lawn-foot to a marsh, between
The treacherous tufts of brighter green,
The garden, plann'd with costly care,
Now wilder'd as a maniac's hair;
The blinded mansion's constant gloom,
Winter and summer, night and day,
Save when the stealthy hours let fall
A sunbeam, or more pallid ray,
Creeping across the floor and wall

From solitary room to room,
To pry and vanish, like the rest,
Weary of a useless quest;
The sombre face of hill and grove,
The very clouds which seem to move
Sadly, be it swift or slow,—
How unlike this, you scarcely know,
Was Southwell Park seven years ago.
Human Spirits, line by line,
Have left hereon their visible trace;
As may, methinks, to Eye Divine,
Human history, and each one's share,
Be closely written everywhere
Over the solid planet's face.
A sour old Witch,—a surly Youth,
Her grandson,—three great dogs, uncouth
To strangers (I'm on terms with all),
Are household now. Sometimes, at fall
Of dusk, a Shape is said to move
Amid the drear entangled grove,
Or seems lamentingly to stand
Beside a pool that's close at hand.
Rare are the human steps that pass
On mossy walk or tufted grass.

   Let's force the brushwood barrier,
No path remaining. Here's a chair!
Once a cool delightful seat,
Now the warty toad's retreat,
Cushion'd with fungus, sprouting rank
Smear'd with the lazy gluey dank.

No doubt the Ghost sits often there—
A Female Shadow with wide eyes
And dripping garments. This way lies
The pool, the little pleasure-lake,
Which cost a pretty sum to make;
Stoop for this bough, and see it **now**
A dismal solitary slough,
Scummy, weedy, ragged, rotten,
Shut in jail, forsook, forgotten.

  Most of the story you have heard:
The bower of bliss at length prepared
To the last blossom, line of gilding,
(**Never** such a dainty building)
One day, **Bride** and Bridegroom came;
The hills at dusk with merry flame
Crowning their welcome: they had June,
Grand weather—and a honeymoon!
Came, to go away too soon,
And never come **again.**
                      The Bride
Was in her old home when she died,
On a winter's day in the time of **snow,**
(She never saw that year to an end),
And he has wander'd far and wide,
And look'd on many a distant hill,
But not on these he used to know,
Round his Park that wave and bend,
And people think he never will.

  Who can probe a spirit's pain?
Who tell that man's loss, or gain?

How far he sinn'd, how far he loved,
How much by what befell was moved,
If there his real happiness
Began, or ended, who shall guess?
Trivial the biographic scroll
Save as a history of the soul,
Perhaps whose mightiest events
Are dumb and secret incidents.
A man's true life and history
Is like the bottom of the sea,
Where mountains and huge valleys hide
Below the wrinkles of the tide,
Under the peaceful mirror, under
Billowy foam and tempest-thunder.
  Rude the flow'r-shrubs' overgrowth ;
Dark frowns the clump of firs beyond ;
At twilight one might well be loth
To linger here alone, and find
The story vivid in one's mind.
A Young Girl, gently bred and fair,
A widow's daughter, whom the Heir
Met somewhere westward on a time,
Came down to this secluded pond,
That's now a mat of weeds and slime,
One summer-day seven years ago,
Sunshine above and flowers below ;
Neglect had driven her to despair ;
And, poor thing, in her frenzied mood
Bursting upon their solitude,
She drown'd herself, before the face

Of Bride and Bridegroom. Here's the place.
   Now mark—that very summer day
You, Ned, and I look'd down this way,
And saw the girl herself—yes, we!
Skirting the coppice—that was She.
   Imagine (this at least is known)
The frantic creature's plunge; the bride
Swooning by her husband's side;
And him, alone, and not alone,
Turning aghast from each to each,
Shouting for help, but none in reach.
He sees the drowning woman sink,
Twice—thrice—then, headlong from the brink,
He drags her to the grass—too late.
There by his servants was he found,
Bewilder'd by the stroke of fate;
With two pale figures on the ground,
One in the chill of watery death,
One with long-drawn painful breath
Reviving. Sudden was the blow,
Dreadful and deep the change. We'll go
And find the house.
                Suspicion pries
From wrinkled mouth and wrinkled eyes,
Deaf dame! Yet constant friends are we,
Or never should I grasp this key,
Or tread this broad and lonely stair
From underground, or let this glare
Of outdoor world insult the gloom
That lives in each forsaken room,

Through which the gammer daily creeps,
And all from dust and mildew keeps.
Few hands may slide this veil aside,
To show—a picture of the Bride.
Is she not gently dignified?
Her curving neck, how smooth and long;
Her eyes, that softly look you through,
To think of violets were to wrong
Their lucency of living blue,
  The new hope of that fair young wife,
The sacred and mysterious life
Which counts as yet no separate hours,
Yielding to sorrow's hurtful powers,
Quench'd its faint gleam before a morn;
And when her breathless babe was born
Almost as still the mother lay,
Almost as dumb, day after day,
Till on the fifth she pass'd away;
And (far too soon) her marriage-bell
Must now begin to ring her knell.
Old man, and child, and village-lass,
Who stood to see her wedding pass—
No further stoops the hoary head,
The merry maid is still unwed,
The child is yet a child, no more,
Watching her hearse go by their door.
Her bridal wreath one summer gave,
The next, a garland for her grave.
  Close the shutter. Bright and sharp
The ray falls on those shrouded things,—

A grand piano and a harp,
Where no one ever plays or sings.
  No, truly,—He will not forget.
But things go on; he's a young man yet;
His life has many a turn to take ;
He may fell this wood, fill up the lake,
Throw down the house (so should not I),
Or sell it to you, Ned, if you'll buy ;
Or, perhaps, come thoughtfully back some day,
With humble heart, and head grown gray.
  Homeward now, as quick as you will ;
These afternoons are short and chill.
There's my haggart, under the hill ;
Through evening's fog the cornstacks rise
Like domes of a little Arab city
Girt by its wall, with a bunch of trees
At a corner—palms, for aught one sees.
Sister Lucy is there alone ;
The good old father and mother gone ;
And I'm not married—more is the pity !
Seem I old bachelor in your eyes ?
—Well, Ned, after dinner to-night,
When a ruddy hearth gives just the light
We used to think best, you'll spread your sail
And carry us far, without wave or gale !
And we'll talk of the old years, and the new,
Of what we have done, and mean to do."

GEORGE HILDEBRAND;

OR, THE SCHOOLFELLOWS.

THE noisy sparrows in our clematis
    Chatted of rain, a pensive summer dusk
Shading the little lawn and garden-ground
Between our threshold and the village-street;
And one pure star, a lonely altar-lamp
In twilight's vast cathedral; for the clouds
Were gravely gathering, and a fitful breeze
Flurried the window-foliage that before
Hung delicately painted on the sky,
And wafted, showering from their golden boss,
The white-rose petals.
              From our garden wall,
Being low within, the great Whiterose-bush lean'd
A thousand tender little heads, to note
The doings of the village all day long;
From when the labourers, trudging to their toil
In earliest sunshine, heard the outpost cocks
Whistle a quaint refrain from farm to farm,
Till hour of shadow, silence, and repose,
The ceasing footstep, and the taper's ray.
Up to the churchyard fence, down to the brook,
And lifted fields beyond with grove and hedge,
The Rose-bush gazed; by-goers on their part,
Feeling a little message of delight

Glanced up to find the sweetness in its bower;
School-children, one arm round a comrade's neck,
Would point to some rich cluster, and repay
Our flying bounty with their happy looks.

In that warm twilight, certain years ago,
At sunset, with the roses in a trance,
And many another blossom fast asleep,
One Flow'r of Flow'rs was closing like the rest.
Night's herald star which look'd across the world
Saw nothing prettier than our little child
Saying his evening prayer at mother's knee,
The white skirt folding on the naked feet,
Too tender for rough ways, his eyes at rest
On his mother's face, a window into heaven.
Kiss'd now, and settled in his cot, he's pleased
With murmuring song, until the large lids droop
Slowly and surely, slumber's regular breath
Not parting the soft mouth. So Annie's boy
And mine was laid asleep. I heard her foot
Stir overhead; and hoped we should have time
Before the rain to loiter half an hour,
As far as to the poplars down the road,
And hear the corncrakes through the meadowy vale,
And watch the childhood of a virgin moon,
Above the faded sunset and its clouds
A floating crescent.
     Sweetheart of my life!—
As then, so now; nay, dearer to me now,
Since love, that fills the soul, expands it too,
And thus it holds more love, and ever more,—

O sweetheart, helpmate, guardian, better self!
Green be those downs and dells above the sea,
Smooth-green for ever, by the plough unhurt,
Nor overdrifted by their neighbouring sands,
Where first I saw you; first since long before
When we were children at an inland place
And play'd together. I had often thought,
I wonder should I know that pleasant child?—
Hardly, I fear'd. I knew her the first glimpse;
While yet the flexile curvature of hat
Kept all her face in shadow to the chin.
And when a breeze to which the harebells danced
Lifted the sun a moment to her eyes,
The ray of recognition flew to mine
Through all the dignity of womanhood.
Like dear old friends we were, yet wondrous new.
The others talk'd; but she and I not much.
Hearing her ribbon whirring in the wind
(No doubting hopes nor whimsies born as yet)
Was pure felicity, like his who sleeps
Within a sense of some unknown good-fortune,
True, or of dreamland, undetermined which;
My buoyant spirit tranquil in its joy
As the white seamew swinging on the wave.
Since, what vicissitude! We read the past
Bound in a volume, catch the story up
At any leaf we choose, and much forget
How every blind to-morrow was evolved,
How each oracular sentence shaped itself
For after comprehension.

                              Thus I mused,
Then also, in that buried summer dusk,
Rich heavy summer, upon autumn's verge,
My wife and boy upstairs, I leaning grave
Against the window; and through favourite paths
Memory, as one who saunters in a wood,
Found sober joy. In turn that eve itself
Rises distinctly. Troops of dancing moths
Brush'd the dry grass. I heard, as if from far,
The tone of passing voices in the street.
Announced by cheerful octaves of a horn,
Those rapid wheels flew, shaking our white-rose,
That link'd us with the modern Magic-Way,
And all the moving million-peopled world.
For every evening, done our share of work,
To keep the threads of life from tanglement,
In happy hour came in the lottery-bag,
Whose messenger had many a prize for us:
The multifarious page ephemeral,
The joy at times of some brave book, whereby
The world is richer; and more special words,
Conveying conjured into dots of ink
Almost the voice, look, gesture that we knew,—
From Annie's former house, or mine, from shore
Of murky Thames, or rarer from hot land
Of Hindoo or Chinese, Canadian woods,
Or that huge isle of kangaroos and gold,
Magnetic metal,—thus on the four winds
One's ancient comrades blown about the world.
Where's George, I thought, our dread, our hope, our p

George Hildebrand, the sultan of the school?
With Greek and Latin at those fingers' ends
That sway'd the winning oar and bat; a prince
In pocket-money and accoutrement;
A Cribb in fist, a Cicero in tongue;
Already victor, when his eye should deign
To fix on any summit of success.
For, in his haughty careless way, he'd hint—
" I've got to push my fortune, by-and-by."
George Hildebrand we worshipp'd, one and all.
But when I went to college he was off,
They said to travel, and he took away
Mentor conjoin'd with Crichton from my hopes,—
No trifling blank. George had done little there,
But could—what could he not? . . And now perhaps,
Some city, in the strangers' burial-ground,
Some desert sand, or hollow under sea,
Hides him without an epitaph. So men
Slip under, fit to shape the world anew;
And leave their trace—in schoolboy memories.

Then I went thinking how much changed I was
Since those old school-times, not so far away,
Yet now like pre-existence. Can that house,
Those fields and trees, be extant anywhere?
Have not all vanish'd, place, and time, and men?
Or with a journey could I find them all,
And myself with them, as I used to be?
Sore was my battle after quitting these.
No one thing fell as plann'd for; sorrows came

And sat beside me; years of toil went round;
And victory's self was pale and garlandless.
Fog rested on my heart; till softly blew
The wind that clear'd it. 'Twas a simple turn
Of life,—a miracle of heavenly love,
For which, thank God!
                        When Annie call'd me up,
We both bent silent, looking at our boy;
Kiss'd unaware (as angels, may be, kiss
Good mortals) on the smoothly rounded cheek,
Turn'd from the window, where a fringe of leaves,
With outlines melting in the darkening blue,
Waver'd and peep'd and whisper'd. Would she walk?
Not yet a little were those clouds to stoop
With freshness to the garden and the field.
I waited by our open door; while bats
Flew silently, and musk geranium-leaves
Were fragrant in the twilight that had quench'd
Or tamed the dazzling scarlet of their blooms.
Peace, as of heaven itself, possess'd my heart.
A footstep, not the light step of my wife,
Disturb'd it; then, with slacker pace, a man
Came up beside the porch. Accosting whom,
And answering to my name: "I fear," he said,
"You'll hardly recollect me now; and yet
We were at school together long ago.
Have you forgotten old George Hildebrand?"

He in the red arm-chair; I not far off,
Excited, laughing, waiting for his face:

The first flash of the candles told me all :
Or, if not all, enough, and more. Those eyes,
When they look'd up at last, were his indeed,
But mesh'd in ugly network, like a snare,
And though his mouth preserved the imperious curve,
Evasion, vacillation, discontent,
Warp'd every feature like a crooked glass.
His hair hung prematurely gray and thin ;
From thread-bare sleeves the wither'd tremulous hands
Protruded. Why paint every touch of blight ?

   Tea came. He hurried into ceaseless talk ;
Glanced at the ways of many foreign towns ;
Knew all those men whose names are on the lip,
And set their worths punctiliously ; brought back
Our careless years ; paid Annie compliments
To spare ; admired the pattern of the cups ;
Lauded the cream,—our dairy's, was it not?
A country life was pleasant, certainly,
If one could be content to settle down ;
And yet the city had advantages.
He trusted, shortly, under his own roof
To practise hospitality in turn.
But first to catch the roof, eh ? Ha, ha, ha !
That was a business topic to discuss
With his old friend—
                For me, I sometimes long'd
To hide my face and groan ; yet look'd at him ;
Opposing pain to grief, presence to thought.

Later, when wine came in, and we two sat
The dreary hours together, how he talk'd !
His schemes of life, his schemes of work and wealth,
Intentions and inventions, plots and plans,
Travels and triumphs, failures, golden hopes.
He was a young man still—had just begun
To see his way. I knew what he could do
If once he tried in earnest. He'd return
To Law, next term but one ; meanwhile complete
His great work, "*The Philosophy of Life;
Or, Man's Relation to the Universe,*"
The matter lying ready to his hand.
Forty subscribers more, two guineas each,
Would make it safe to publish. All this time
He fill'd his glass and emptied, and his tongue
Went thick and stammering. When the wine came in
(Perhaps a blame for me—who knows?) I saw
The glistening eye ; a thin and eager hand
Made the decanter chatter on the glass
Like ague. Could I stop him? So at last
He wept, and moan'd he was a ruin'd man,
Body and soul ; then cursed his enemies
By name, and promised punishment ; made vaunt
Of genius, learning ; caught my hand again,—
Did I forget my friend—my dear old friend ?
Had I a coat to spare ? He had no coat
But this one on his back ; not one shirt—see !

'Twas all a nightmare ; all plain wretched truth.
And how to play physician ? Where's the strength

Repairs a slow self-ruin from without?
The fall'n must climb innumerable steps,
With humbleness, and diligence, and pain.
How help him to the first of all that steep?

 Midnight was past. I had proposed to find
A lodging near us; for, to say the truth,
I could not bid my wife, for such a guest
In such a plight, prepare the little room
We still call'd " Emma's " from my sister's name.
Then with a sudden mustering up of wits,
And ev'n a touch of his old self, that quick
Melted my heart anew, he signified
His bed was waiting, he would say good-night,
And begg'd me not to stir, he knew his road.
But arm in arm I brought him up the street,
Among the rain-pools, and the pattering drops
Drumming upon our canopy; where few
Or none were out of doors; and once or twice
Some casement from an upper story shed
Penurious lamplight.   Tediously we kept
The morning meal in vain expectancy.
Our box of clothes came back; the people said
He paid without a word, and went his way,
They knew not whither. He return'd no more.
He now is dead.   Through all the summer-time
The touch of that unhappy visit lay,
Like trace of frost on gardens, on our life.

Great cities give events to every hour;
Not so that ancient village, small, remote,
Half-hid in boscage of a peaceful vale,
With guardian hills, but welcoming the sun,
And every group of seasonable stars
That rises on the circle of the year;
Open to natural influences; far
From jostling crowds of congregated men.
  That village also lies behind us now;
Midst other fields abide we, other faces.
Annie, my darling, we were happy there,
And Heaven continues happiness and hope
To us and to our children. May their steps
Keep the good pathway through this perilous world.
That village is far-off, that year is fled.
But still, at many a meditative hour
By day or night, or with memorial flash,
I see the phantom of George Hildebrand,
A shifting ghost,—now with his boyhood's face
And merry curls; now haggard and forlorn,
As when the candles came into the room.

  One sells his soul; another squanders it;
The first buys up the world, the second starves,
Poor George was loser palpably enough;
Supernal Wisdom only knows how much.

MERVAUNEE.

Part I.

WHEN summer days are hot and blue,
How well for thee that may'st pursue,
Far from the city's crowded street,
The winding brook with wandering feet,
Conquer the mountain's airy crest,
Lose thee in woodland glade; or, best,
Breathe ocean-wind where curl'd waves roar;
Swim from the land, or lie at rest
To watch mid noonday light's repose
Cloud-shadows cross the mighty floor,
Or plighted crimsons in the west
When soft the lazy ripple flows
Like sleep upon a wearied brain.

Suppose it thus; suppose thee fain
Of song or story, some wild thing
Reported from the mystic main,—
Of Dalimar now hear me sing,
Son of a long-forgotten king.

King Erc the Fortunate was dead,
And Diarmad ruled the clans instead,
Of West Ierné, strong in war,
Generous in peace; and Dalimar,
His younger brother, dwelt with him.
Nor show'd the sun and moonlight dim

"Ierné," Ancient Ireland.

In those long-faded seasons; bright
Was many a fresh new morrow's light
Along the mountains, evening gold
Fell on the wave, in times of old.
   Their **Fortress-Hill**, a mighty mound,
With houses built of the strong oak-tree,
Entrench'd and palisaded round,
Ring within ring, o'erlook'd the sea
And rugged woods of wolf and bear;
A land of gloomy pathways, where
Wild men crept also to and fro
To snatch a prey with club and bow;
Till sharply blew the signal-horn
The warriors of the Rath to warn,
And bid them drive the plunderers back
With blood upon their hasty track.
Or sometimes ocean-rovers fierce
Dared with their waspish navy pierce
A river-mouth or guardless bay
And sting the land with fire and sword;
Then sped the warriors forth, to slay
And chase and scatter, and drive aboard.
   But when the battle spoil was won,
Or when the hunting-day was done,
They heard, o'er fragrant cups of mead,
Their Bards rehearse each daring deed
To ringing harps, or duly count
Those high ancestral steps that mount

" Rath," a Keltic fortress.

To Balor and to Parthalon,
Or some thrice-famous story tell
Of war, or dark Druidic spell
(To-day no weaker), or how well
A Spirit loved a mortal Youth;
And all was heard and held for truth.

Archpoet Conn was old and blind.
No whiter to the autumnal wind
Marsh-cotton waves on rushy moor
Than flow'd his hair and beard, and pure
His raiment when he sat in hall
As torrent-foam or seagull's breast.
The King, in seven rich colours drest,
Pledged him at feast and festival,
And gladly to his master's voice
Conn bow'd the snowy sightless head.
Young Dalimar, in robe of red,
Sat next the Bard, of kindly choice,
And spake to him and carved his dish,
And fill'd the goblet to his wish,
That love for loss might make amends;
For youth and age were steadfast friends.
And many a time with careful hand
He led the Sage to the salt sea-sand,
Slow-pacing by the murmurous flood,
Or to a shelter'd glen where stood
One sacred oak-tree, broad and low,

" Balor and Parthalon," two mythic heroes.

Firm as the rocks that saw it grow,
A cromlech, and a pillar-stone.
And, year by year, of things unknown
He learn'd.
 In shadow of that oak
Conn taught the Prince of fairy-folk
Who dwell within the hollow hills,
In founts of rivers and of rills,
In caves and woods, and some that be
Underneath the cold green sea;
The spells they cast on mortal men,
And spells to master these again;
And Dalimar all that strange lore
Longing heard and lonely ponder'd,
Musing, wondering, as he wander'd
Through the forest or by the shore.
And when his elder Brother said,
" My Brother, with the brow of care!
O Dalimar! I rede thee, wed;
No lack of noble maids and fair;"—
Ever the younger Chief replied,
"Yea—but I have not seen my bride,
Though many beauties; when I see,
Know her I shall, and she know me."
—" I dread lest thou have turn'd thy mind
To something man may never find,
Some love the wide earth cannot give."
—" So must I ever loveless live!"

" Cromlech," a kind of stone sepulchre.

Nor thought his pensive fortune hard,
Communing with the wise old Bard.
 But winter came, and Conn no more
Slow enter'd hall, or paced on sand,
Or sat in shadow of oaktree bough;
If you should search the sea and land
You could not find his white head now,
Unless beneath a cairn of stones
Where round Slieve Rann the north-wind moans.
And young Prince Dalimar thought long
The nights of darkness.; tale or song,
Or maiden's eyes, to youth so dear,
Banquet, or jest, or hunting-spear,
He nothing prized, or warrior-fame
Once green with promise round his name.
Though gentle, he could wield a sword,
And plunge into the waves of war;
Lorcan, who spake an evil word,
Hand to hand in fight he slew;
And when a wildboar overthrew
His elder brother, Dalimar
Sprang from his horse with ready knife
And found the fierce brute's throbbing life
In one sharp stroke. But weary pass'd
Midwinter now. The barren sea
Roar'd, and the forest roar'd, and he
Was lonely in his thoughts.
      At last
One day 'twas spring. Dim swelling buds
Thicken'd the web of forest boughs,

Bird and beast began to arouse,
Caper'd and voiced in glad relief;
The salmon cleft the river-floods,
The otter launch'd from his hole in the bank,
Away went the wild swans' airy rank
From salt lagoon; far out on the reef
The seals lay basking; broadly bright
Ocean glitter'd in morning light;
And the young Chief sprang to his little boat
And paddled away on the deep afloat,
By dreadful precipice and cave,
Where slumbers now the greedy wave
Lull'd by that blue heav'n above.

   Then, so it chanced, his coracle
Glided into a rocky cove
And up a lonely little strand;
And out he stept on sunny sand
Whereon a jagged shadow fell
From the steep o'erhanging cliff,
And drew ashore his fragile skiff.

   What spies he on the tawny sand?
A cold sea-jelly, cast away
By fling of ebbing water?——nay!
A little Cap, of changeful sheen,
A seamless Cap of rippled green
Mingling with purple like the hue
Of ocean weeds.
               He stoop'd; its touch
Like thinnest lightning ran him through
With blissful shiver, sharp and new!

What might it mean? for never such
A chance had come to Dalimar;
He felt as when, in dream, a star
Flew to him, bird-like, from the sky.

   But then he heard a sad low cry,
And, turning, saw five steps away—
Was it a Woman?—strange and bright,
With long loose hair, and her body fair
Shimmering as with watery light;
For nothing save a luminous mist
Of tender beryl and amethyst
Over the living smoothness lay,
Statue-firm from head to feet,—
A breathing Woman, soft and sweet,
And yet not earthly.
                So she stood
One marvellous moment in his sight;
Then, lapsing to another mood,
Her mouth's infantine loveliness
Trembling pleaded in sore distress;
Her wide blue eyes with great affright
Were fill'd; two slender hands she press'd
Against the roundlings of her breast,
Then with a fond face full of fears
She held them forth, and heavy tears
Brimm'd in silence and overflow'd.
He, doubting much what this might be,
Watch'd her.
         Swiftly pointed she;
Utter'd some sound of foreign speech;

But Dalimar held out of reach
The Cap, behind-back,—and so each
Regarded other.
                    Then she flung
Her arms aloft,—stood straight,—her wide
Eyes gazed on his, and into him;
And she began a solemn song,
Of words uncouth, slow up and down;
A song that deepen'd as she sung,
That soon was loud and swift and strong
Like the rising of a tide,
With power to seize and drench and drown
The senses,—till his sight grew dim,
A torpor crept on every limb.
What could he do?—an ocean-spell
Was on him.
                    But old wisdom rush'd
Into his mind, and with a start,
One gasp of breath, one leap of heart,
He pluck'd his dagger from its sheath,
Held forth the little Cap beneath
Its glittering point. The song was hush'd.
Prone on the yellow sand she fell.
  He kneels, he takes her hands, with gentle,
Tender, passionate words—in vain;
Then with a heart of love and pain
Wraps her in his crimson mantle,
Lifts her, lays her down with care,
As she a one-year infant were,
Within his woven coracle,

And o'er the smooth sea guides it well,
And bears her up the rocky path,
And through the circles of the Rath,
To Banva's bower, his sister dear.
There, half in pity, half in fear,
The women tend her, till she sighs
And opens wide her wondrous eyes.
   Dalimar alone of all
In his deep heart understood
Of this Damsel dimly bright
Wafted from the salt-sea flood;
Like a queen when cloth'd aright.
Only a little web, more light
Than any silk, that halfway goes
Between the fingers and the toes,
Her under-ocean breeding shows.
She hath wept and ceased to weep;
Slow her wearied eyelids fall;
Lay her softly, let her sleep.

" Bright and strange One, where wert found?
    (Sleep! while Banva sings)
From caves and waves of the fishful sea,
From swell and knell of the rolling tide,
    (Slumber! while we sing to thee)
Borne forlorn to our fortress-mound—
    (Sleep! while Banva sings).
Fairest maiden, sea-blue-eyed,
Sea-shell-tinted, thy unbound

And wavy-flowing hair is dried
And comb'd away on either side,
    (While Banva sings, and Derdra sings)
Down from smoothly pillow'd head;
Safe art thou on shadowy bed,
Sleep now—safe art thou
    In the Dune of Kings."

She slept. They heard a thrush outside
Clear across vernal woods, the tide
Searching among his rocks below,
And the spearman pacing to and fro.

MERVAUNEE.

PART II.

ALONG the level sands I heard
    The mystic water, how it stirr'd
And whisper'd of the days of old;
While Sun touch'd ocean, sank,—and soon
Eastwards a tawny vaporous Moon
Rose ghostlike, to that solemn tune
Of waves. A path of ruddy gold,
Of yellow gold, in turn unroll'd
Full to my feet. Without a word,
I heard an ancient story told.

  A Princess of the Sea, a Prince
Of the West Isle,—and never since

" Dune " was a rath of importance.

Was any fairer couple wed
Or loved each other more.   As fled
Month after month, year after year,
Their love grew every day more dear,
Glad, sad, together, or apart;
Tender they were, and true of heart.
 Askest what love is?   Hast thou known
Love's true religion? from thy own
Learn all true lovers' creed; there is
No other way to learn but this.
The best things thou hast found or dream'd—
Howso they new and special seem'd,
Most intimately thine,—are part
Of Man's inheritance; thou art
Co-heir with many.   That bright Road,
Where only wingèd Fancy trode,
Stretch'd on the wave by moon or sun,
Did over darkling waters run
Directly to the gazer's feet,—
And was not thus; and yet no cheat.
If any radiancy divine
Doth straight into thy spirit shine,
Lo, it is thine—not singly thine.
The wondrous light that shone to thee
A child, the children saw, and see;
And Love's wide-spread celestial glow
To each peculiarly doth flow.
If thou hast been a lover, so
These loved in bye-gone days.

                              Befell
One spring-day, from the circling mound,
Where her Sun-chamber builded well
Look'd wide on all the prospect round,
Princess **Mervaunee** watch'd the sea,—
Her two **young sons beside her** knee.
Her solemn eyes of changeful blue
Larger, it seem'd, and darker grew,
And mournful as they never were
Till now. The children gazed on her,
With awe of that strange mournfulness,
The sense whereof they might not guess.
But youth still turns to thoughts of joy,
And quickly spake the younger Boy,
" O Mother! would we had a boat
Upon these merry waves afloat,
To sail away and leave the land!"
The elder Brother shouted—" I
Would dive beneath the waves, and spy
Who live there!"
                              Nothing did she say,
But stared upon them, seized a hand
Of each, and hurried them away.
Then, to her husband, " Grant me grace!"
She said, " and take me from this place!
The moaning restless water kills
All peace within me, day or night,
And soon will be my death outright;
Take me to inland woods and hills.
I love the quiet grassy earth,

Calm lakes, tree-shadows, wild birds' mirth,
I hate this heaving watery floor,
Its ceaseless voices, more and more.
Take me away!—O love, forgive!"
He marvell'd; but he loved her best
Of all things, and on this behest
Sought out an inland place to live.

   Amid the hills, wide-forested,
With rocky pastures interspread,
The sky is in a placid lake,
Steep-shored, transparent-water'd, lonely,—
A bed of reeds at one place only,
'Twixt the water and the brake.
There, driving many an oaken stake
Into the shallow, skilful hands
A steadfast island-dwelling make,
Seen from the hill-tops like a fleet
Of wattled houses; beams of oak
Fix them; and soon a light-blue smoke
Goes up across the crowd of trees,
Where greening Spring is busy anew,
Dark holly intermixt, and yew,
And here and there a hoary rock.

   The wolf, the wild-cat, and the bear
Prowl'd in these woods or made their lair;
Strange yells at midnight came, or oft
At dead of night,—while safe and soft
Within their Island-Houses slept,
On rushy mat and woollen cloak
And fur of beast, the Prince's folk,

Save who in turn the nightwatch kept;
The Prince himself, and Mervaunee,
And two brave Boys, where they should be;
While, underneath, the ripple crept,
And morning rose behind the hills.

  There bide they while the Spring refills
Earth's cup with **life-wine** to the brink,
And every creature joys to drink.
They fish'd, they hunted, ranged afar
Through labyrinthine woods, made war
On catamount and cruel wolf;
And, three times, Dalimar himself
Spear-smote the spreading-antler'd elk
And dash'd **to** ground his mighty bulk.
They drove the milky kine to feed
In forest lawn and marshy mead,
Or swam their wolf-hounds, pure **of breed,**
Or hollow'd the tree-trunk for canoe,
Made nets **and lines, and** bows **of yew,**
Goblets, and other things of wood
For a hundred **uses** good,
Nor bare of carving. Mervaunee,
Span with her tall handmaidens three,
Taught her sons whate'er she could,
Tended the household well, prepared
The evening feast which all folk shared;
Then gladly heard the minstrel sing
His tales, or touch'd herself the string
(But seldom this) to music strange
Floating through many a subtle change.

Thus fled the summertime away.
  "Art thou at peace?" he said one day,
Kissing her lips. "O Dalimar!
Lovest me yet? Thou dost, I know,
But still I'd have thee tell me so!"
"I loved thee first ten years ago;
And now I love thee better far.
Nay, thou hast kept thy bloom of youth
All perfect."
        "Dalimar, in sooth,
There is my sorrow! I can see
A touch or two of time on thee,
Dearer for this,—but—may thy wife
Now tell thee somewhat of the life
Of those beneath the waves, and teach
What I have always shunn'd in speech,
Nay shunn'd in thought?—but year by year
Brings the inevitable near.

  "In those vast kingdoms under sea,
Dusky at noontide, some there be
Of mine, a magic race, that dwell,
And how we came there none can tell,
Imperial mid the monstrous forms
Of Ocean's creeping, gliding swarms;
We live three hundred years or more,
Three hundred years, and sometimes four,
And then—ah misery!—and then—

  "I said, it is not so with men
Of that bright Upper World, who breathe
Crystalline ether, live beneath

The great dominion of the Sun
And Starry Night—(O Night with Stars!).
Sure nothing there, I said, debars
Or daunts them, be it life or death,
Inspired with such transcendent breath,
And clear Infinity **begun!**

  "Fearful our visits, short and rare
To your unbounded World of Air,
By an old secret, told to few,
And perilous of proof. I knew
The danger, but I loved **it** too;
And sometimes, **good** or evil hap,
Would even doff that precious Cap
Which all beneath the sea must wear,
Because I thus felt greater share
Of earth-life, an unwonted sense
Of fearful hope and joy intense
Commingling,—seem'd almost to rise
And float immortal through those skies
Without a limit.
                "I have proved
Earth's **life and love,** through thee, Belov'd,
And through thee, happy. Former days
Withdrew into a distant haze;
First I had Thee, then twofold bliss,
And threefold: better lot than this
Heart could not dream of—might it stay.

  "**It** smote me suddenly one day,
Like arrow from an unseen bow,
A poison'd arrow—He must go,

And thou remain! He shall wax old
Ere fifth part of thy life be told,
And die, and leave thee desolate,
With all the endless years to wait!
My sons too—'tis not death I fear;
If we all die, then death is dear;
But long sad lonely life. O Sea,
At least thou hast a death for me!
Nay, husband, kiss me, clasp me tight,
Albeit I lack the human right
Of growing old along with thee!"

She wept; he sooth'd her as he could,
And cheer'd her to a brighter mood.
But grief came shadowing back; and when
Dark autumn gain'd on wood and fen
She felt the moaning of the trees
Was worse to suffer than the sea's.
"It taunts us with the distant shore—
Return we!"
    They return'd. Once more
The salt gale stirr'd her robes and hair,
But could not breathe away her care;
The trouble grew, the sad unrest,
And most of all when moony nights
Whiten'd the surf, or spread afar
O'er lonely tracts of sea. His best
Of comforting tried Dalimar;
Beyond the hour availing nought,
For in their lives a change was wrought.

One dreary afternoon, while She
Sat gazing on the doleful sea,
She saw her Husband by her stand,
The Cap of Magic in his hand,
His face was ashy, his voice low
And hollow, and his words came slow:
"My strange dear Lady of the Sea,
If thou hast mind to part from me
And live no longer on the land,
Take this, and let thy choice be free."
She did not speak, she did not look;
As in a trance the Cap she took.
At its touch a tremor shook
Suddenly through her, from head to feet,
And back she lay in the carven seat,
With staring eyes and visage wan,
As though she were at point to die;
Then started up with sudden cry—
"O Dalimar!"—but he was gone.

And none saw Her go; nor found trace;
Nor henceforth look'd upon her face.
From that hour, empty was her place.

On a winter night, when the fire burn'd brig
After flocks of years had flown away,
Voiceful O'Kennedy sung his lay,
And his yearning harp was tuned aright
For ripples of music that keep afloat
The little tale like a gliding boat:

"Who will hearken to harp and rhyme,
Of things that befell in olden time?"

"For one more voyage Prince Dalimar sail'd;
 His two bold sons in the ship with him;
  Though his beard was white, and his eyesight dim,
   And his strength was fail'd.
(Hush a little for harp and rhyme:
This befell in the olden time.)

"Weary was he with endless quest
 By watery way and island bay;
  Never seeing by night or day
   One he loved best.
(Hush a little for harp and rhyme:
This befell in the olden time.)

"For he had wedded a fairy wife,
 And she had left him, he knew not why,
  And till he had found her he would not die,
   Though sad was life.
(Hush a little for harp and rhyme:
This befell in the olden time.)

"A sunset over mid-ocean spread,
 Where the ship, becalm'd, did gently sway;
  And there on deck Prince Dalimar lay,
   As well-nigh dead.
(Hush a little for harp and rhyme:
This befell in the olden time.)

" Closed were his eyes, and pallid his face,
    His sons and his sailors standing round ;
    They thought ' He is far from the burial-mound
        Of his chieftain-race.'
(Hush a little for harp and rhyme :
This befell in the olden time.)

" But he opens his eyes, he lifts his hands,
    Like one who sees some wonderful sight ;
    He raises himself, his eyes grow bright ;
        Straight up he stands!
(Hush a little for harp and rhyme :
This befell in the olden time.)

" He sighs, ' Long-while have I lived alone.'
    He smiles, ' It is Thou !' and then, with one lea
    Into the heave of the glassy deep,
        Sinks like a stone.
(Hush a little for harp and rhyme :
This befell in the olden time.)

" Swifter than cormorants plunged the men,
    Rose for breath, and dived anew ;
    But they swam to the ship when dark it grew,
        All silent then.
(Hush a little for harp and rhyme :
This befell in the olden time.)

" Voyaging homewards, often a gleam
    Encompass'd the vessel, and with the light
    A waft of music. One still midnight
        There came a Dream.

(Hush a little for harp and rhyme :
This befell in the olden time.)

" At full moon, full tide,—to each Brother the same :
  His Father and Mother, hand in hand,
  Immortally fair, beside him stand,
    And speak his name.
(Hush a little for harp and rhyme :
This befell in the olden time.)

" Seeming out of the water to rise,
  Enclosed in a radiant atmosphere,
  And to float aloft, and disappear
    Into the skies.
(Hush a little for harp and rhyme :
This befell in the olden time.)

" The ship sail'd fast in the morning sun
  By point and cave, as the fair wind blew,
  And into a little port she knew,
    And her voyage was done.
(Hush a little for harp and rhyme :
This befell in the olden time.)

" Where the mounded Rath overlooks the sea
  The Pillar-Stone is a beacon afar ;
  Graven in ogham, ' DALIMAR—
    MERVAUNEE.'
(This was all in the olden time ;
And here is the end of harp and rhyme.)"

But this too is a byegone song.
The Rath has been for ages long
A grassy hill; the Standing-stone
Looks on a country bare and lone,
And lonelier billows,—half a word
Of ogham at the edge, all blurr'd
With crust of lichens yellow and gray.
There you may sit of a summer day,
And watch the white foam rise and fall
On rampart cliffs of Donegal,
And the wild sheep on the greensward stray,
And the sea-line sparkle far away.

I KNOW not if it may be mine
To add a song, nay, half a line,
To that fair treasure-house of wit,
That more than cedarn cabinet,
Where men preserve their precious things,
Free wealth, surpassing every king's.
I only know, I felt and wrote
According to the day and hour,
According to my little power;
Unskill'd to break and weigh and measure
The World's materials—as it seem'd
Lovely, I loved it, worshipp'd, dream'd,
And sung, for sadness or for pleasure.
If souls unborn shall take some note
Or none at all, 'tis their affair;
I cannot guess, and will not care.
Yet hoping still that something done
Has so much life from earth and sun,
Drawn through man's finer brain, as may
In mystic form, with mystic force,
Reach forward from a fleeting day,
But a profound perennial source,
To touch upon his earthly way
Some brother pilgrim-soul, and say
(A whisper in the wayside grass)—
" I have gone by, where now you pass;
" Been sorely tried with frost and heat,
" With stones that bruise the weary feet,

" With crag and quag, with fire and flood,
" With desert sands that parch the blood ;
" Nor fail'd to find a flowery dell,
" A shady grove, a crystal well :
" And I am gone, thou know'st not whither.
" —Thou thyself art hastening thither.
" Thou hast thy life ; and nothing can
" Have more.   Farewell, O Brother Man !"

NOTES.

NOTES.

Note A.

A good many of the lyrics in this volume have been published with music, but in no case has an exclusive right been given, and the copyright of all (for publication with music or otherwise) remains entirely in the hands of the author. The following were written to Irish tunes:—"The Winding Banks of Erne;" "The Girl's Lamentation;" "Among the Heather;" "The Bright Little Girl;" "Kate of Ballyshanny;" "Lovely Mary Donelly;" "The Milkmaid;" "The Nobleman's Wedding." Although the use of words and phrases not in general use has been avoided, some Irishisms have naturally slipt in; all, I think, explained in the Notes; and one unusual spelling is risked (perhaps rashly)—"redd" for the past tense of read; a change being certainly wanted. The word "red" carries a strong colour, and ought not to have more to do.

Note B (page 3).

"In a Broken Tower." This has hitherto been called "Wayconnell Tower," and I am sorry that Mr. Longfellow has been misled by the name to include it in his *Poems of Places—Ireland*. It was only a *fancy* name, the "locus in quo" (really one of the towers of Conway Castle) being altogether subsidiary; and it is better fitted with a less special title,—like "The Ruined Chapel" (which belongs by birth to a secluded little ruin on the shore of Killybegs Harbour) and a great many other pieces in this volume. "The Winding Banks of Erne" and "Abbey Asaroe" are local pieces proper.

Note B 2 (page 111).

"Galloglas"—"kern"—native Irish foot-soldiers; the first heavy-armed, the second light.

Note C (page 136).

Abbey Asaroe. At the head of a small creek in Ballyshannon Harbour, in an old and crowded graveyard, stand or crumble the ruins of this Abbey of the Cistercian Order, founded in or about the year 1178, by Roderick O'Cananan, Prince of Tirconnell.— (Archdall, *Monas. Hib.*) Only some venerable dark-gray fragments of wall remain. "The windows are shapeless gaps; weeds and old ragged bushes grow in the aisle; many of the stones are built into the wall of fishermen's huts, or help to fence their scanty potato patches, while pieces of archivolts, mullions, and other carved work, are more reverently set for headstones in the neighbouring graveyard."

The Abbey took its name from the waterfall. More than 2,500 years ago, say the oldest histories, Aedh Ruadh (Red Hugh), High-King of Erin, was drowned in the river Erne—swept away, it would seem, in attempting to cross by one of the fords. He "was buried in the mound over the margin of the cataract" [*Donegal Annals*, Anno Mundi 4518]. Hence *Eas-Aedha-Ruaidh*, "Waterfall of Red Hugh," written in English in various ways, of which "Asaroe" has been here fixed on.

Note D (page 138).

The Lupracaun (pronounced Lup-ragh-aun, *gh* guttural) is an elf peculiar to Ireland, and known, with some variations of name, in every part of the country,—the Fairy Shoemaker who may be forced to give you of his store of gold, *if* you can keep your eye on him. Mr. Keightley (*Fairy Mythology*) thinks the word is the same as the English "Lubberkin." In O'Reilly's Ir.-Eng. Dict. we find "Lobaircin, a dwarf."

Note E (page 141).

"The Winding Banks of Erne." The important river Erne rises in Lough Gowna, not very far from the middle of Ireland, and, after a course of some seventy miles through a chain of islanded lakes, pours its foaming waters over the Fall of Asaroe into Ballyshannon Harbour on Donegal Bay. The name of Ballyshannon is corrupt, both in the "Bally" and the "Shannon;" the Irish form is *Bel-atha-Seanaigh*, and the people call it, properly, "Bellashanny," or often, by way of compromise, "Ballyshanny," which last I have adopted as not too much disguising the legally established, though corrupt, name. Bellashannay would be more euphonious. *Bel atha* means literally "Mouth or Opening of the Ford;" but the compound, which is common in Irish names, seems to have no other significance than *Ath* by itself, and merely to signify "ford." *Sean* means "old" (senex), but *Seanaigh* is probably a man's name; Seanach or Shannagh in the possessive case. *Ath-seanaigh* (Shannagh's Ford?) was a ford a little above the present bridge, and by this name the town and castle are usually designated in the Irish Annals. A general account of this locality will be found in *Rambles*, by Patricius Walker, chapters v. and vi.

Note F (page 156).

"The Nobleman's Wedding." My dear George Petrie sent me an imperfect and corrupt version of this ballad, taken down from the singing of a nurse in his family, and I put it into its present form for his *Ancient Music of Ireland*.

Note G (page 171).

"The Dirty Old Man." A singular man, named Nathaniel Bentley, for many years kept a large hardware shop in Leadenhall Street, London. He was best known as "Dirty Dick" (Dick for alliteration's sake, probably), and his place of business as "the Dirty Warehouse." He died about the year 1809. The verses accord with the accounts respecting himself and his house. Some twelve or fifteen years ago I saw a placard in the window of a coffee-house in Leadenhall Street,—" Formerly the residence of the celebrated Dirty Dick." But the original house had then been made into two. A woodcut of Dirty Dick's shop is given in *Willis's Current Notes.*

"The Dirty Old Man," and "The Schoolfellows" (p. 295), were first published in Mr. Dickens's *Household Words*, and I believe had the honour of suggesting to the great novelist something in *Great Expectations* and in *A Tale of Two Cities* respectively.

Note H (page 179).

"The Ballad of Squire Curtis." I dreamed the supernatural incident. The supposed authority for the whole story is as good as that offered for a great many ghost-stories.

Note I (page 191).

"King Henry's Hunt." Waltham was in the time of Henry the Eighth a woody district, which included the present "Epping Forest." The tradition of this particular hunt is traceable up to the time of Elizabeth. It has been sometimes claimed for Richmond Park, but, as far as I know, against all the evidence.

Note J (p. 215).

"Cape Ushant." A real incident. The day was Sunday, the 23rd of July, 1815. See Captain Maitland's *Narrative of the Surrender of Bonaparte*, p. 109 (London: Colburn, 1826), also *Memoirs of an Aristocrat, and Anecdotes of Napoleon* (London: Whittaker, 1837).

Note K (page 305).

Mervaunee. This is a coined name, founded on the "Merrow," or sea-maiden of Irish tradition. Her cap was called *Cohuleen Driuth*—magical (Druidic?) little cap or cowl.

The scene of the poem is laid in Pagan Ireland, for which

Ierne [Western Land?] was one of the names. Parthalon and Balor are two of the traditional ancestors of the Irish; Parthalon, a Greek who landed with a small body of colonists on the Island of the West; Balor, a giant, with one eye in the middle of his forehead and one in the back of his head.

Raths were the usual habitations of the wealthier; they were very numerous, and varied much in size, the most important getting the name of Dūn. A Rath occupied a hill or mound, and consisted of circular earthworks palisaded, enclosing the wooden dwellings, cattle byres, &c. Remains of the mounds are very common all over Ireland; and are just the same in character as the "British Camps" and "Rings" in England.

Lake-houses, mostly of wood, on artificial islands, were anciently very numerous in Ireland, and are often spoken of in the *Annals*. The island was commonly made by a ring of oaken piles filled in with stones, earth, &c. The Irish name of such a dwelling-place is *Crannog* (*Crann* is "a tree"). The first examined in modern times was that of Lagore, properly Loch Gabhair, County Meath, in or about the year 1839; since when by the drainage of lakes, many others have been found. A good account of the crannoges is given by Sir William Wilde in the Royal Irish Academy Museum Catalogue (ut supra), pp. 220-235.

In 1853-4 very similar structures were discovered in Switzerland, the water being unusually low, in the Lakes of Zurich, Biel, Sempach, Neufchatel, and Geneva. Some of these have been described by Professor F. Keller, under the name of *Keltische Pfahlbauten* (Trans. Antiq. Soc. Zurich, vol. ix.).

Note L (page 325).

Ogham (spelt also "Ogum" and "Oguim," the ō apparently always long—I cannot find any etymology—) is an ancient kind of writing, of which a dozen or more examples, monumental inscriptions on stones, may be seen in the Museum of the Royal Irish Academy, Dublin. The greater number of those discovered in Ireland have been found in Kerry and Cork; a few have been noticed in Wales and Scotland, and one in Shetland. The Rev. Charles Graves, who has specially studied the subject, says, "The Ogham alphabet consists of lines, or groups of lines, variously arranged with reference to a single stem-line, or to an edge of the substance on which they are traced. The spectator, looking at an upright Ogham monument, will in general observe groups of incised strokes of *four* different kinds:—(1) groups of lines to the left; (2) others to the right of the edge; (3) other longer strokes crossing it obliquely; and (4) small notches upon the edge itself."—(Catalogue of the Museum of the Royal Irish Academy: "Stone, Earthen, and Vegetable Materials," page 137.) Several questions regarding the Ogham characters are still in debate amongst the learned, some arguing for their immense antiquity; it appears certain, however, that they were in use after the Christian era.

Note M.

The sympathetic reader may be trusted to see that the division into "Day and Night Songs" and "Songs and Ballads," is not arbitrary; and also that the word "Songs" is not always or generally used in the strictest sense. But here and there comes a Song proper.

INDEX.

	PAGE
Adieu to Ballyshanny! where I was bred and born	141
A fair witch crept to a young man's side	32
A fire keeps burning in this breast	284
After the long bitter days, and nights weigh'd down with my sadness	38
A gentle face and clear blue eyes	55
A golden pen I mean to take	85
All hail to our Mountain! form well-known!	45
Along the level sands I heard	314
A man there came, whence none can tell	201
A messenger, that stood beside my bed	36
A schooner's in the bay	212
A shadowy fringe the fir-trees make	89
At me one night the angry moon	109
Autumnal night's deep azure dome	198
A venerable white-hair'd Man	179
Bare twigs in April enhance our pleasure	112
Beautiful, beautiful Queen of the Forest	100
Birdie, Birdie, will you pet?	165
Bud and leaflet, opening slowly	7
But few days gone	57
By the shore, a plot of ground	18
Came north and south and east and west	183
Checquer'd with woven shadows as I lay	70
Come again, delightful Spring	104
Death stately came to a young man, and said	92
Doleful was the land	63
Down on the shore, on the sunny shore!	169

INDEX.

	PAGE
Fairies and **Elves**!	260
Far from the churchyard **dig his grave**	104
Flee from London, good my **Walter**!	121
For many a day, like one whose **limbs are stiff**	95
Friend Edward, from this turn remark	277
God save you, **Goodman** Dodd,—a sight to see you!	186
Goodbye, goodbye **to Summer**!	168
Good evening. Why, of course it's you!	196
Good Lord, to thee I bow my head	118
Gray, gray is Abbey Asaroe	136
Greet thee kindly, Wayside Well	25
Head the ship for England!	209
Hear you **now a throbbing wind that calls**	102
Heave at the windlass!—Heave O, cheerly, men!	208
Her blue eyes they beam and they twinkle	11
Here the white-ray'd anemone is born	16
His Town is one of memory's haunts	91
I built my castle upon the sea-side	160
I dream'd that I, being dead a hundred years	77
I heard the dogs howl in the moonlight night	14
I know, I see, that you are fair	34
I know not if it may be mine	327
I'm glad I am alive, to see and feel	52
In a dirty old house lived a **Dirty Old Man**	171
In a grove I saw one day	19
In little German Weimar	52
In trouble for my sin, I cried to God	66
I sat at home, and thought there lived no green	60
I scatter the dreams of my pillow	69
I see two children **hush'd to death**	67
Is it all in vain?	29
I strove for wicked peace, **but might not win**	94
I thought it was **the** little bed	59
It is a careless pretty may, down **by yon river-side**	205
I walk'd in the lonesome **evening**	10

King Henry stood in Waltham Wood	191
Lady fair, lady fair	78
Let all your looks be grave and cold	24
Let us not teach and preach so much	61
Little Cowboy, what have you heard	138
Long ago,—a little girl	162
Moaning blast	77
Music and Love!—If lovers hear me sing	221
No longer any choice remains	117
Now, at the hour when ignorant mortals	71
Now Autumn's fire burns slowly along the woods	38
Now fare-you-well! my bonny ship	214
Now is Queen Autumn's progress through the land	74
Now let me choose a native blossom	40
Now what doth Lady Alice so late on the turret stair	199
October—and the skies are cool and gray	45
O'er western tides the fair Spring Day	86
Oh, hearing sleep, and sleeping hear	23
O how dimly walks the wisest	95
Oh, lovely Mary Donnelly, it's you I love the best!	131
Oh! were my Love a country lass	16
O Maryanne, you pretty girl	9
O nameless Fear, which I would fain contemn!	94
On a sunny Saturday evening	79
Once I was guest at a Nobleman's wedding	156
One evening walking out, I o'ertook a modest *colleen*	155
On the Longest Day	50
O pale green sea	63
O Spirit of the Summertime!	102
O unknown Belov'd One! to the mellow season	30
Our ship, the stout Bellerophon	215
Out of the city, far away	4
O welcome! friendly stars, one by one, two by two	115
O where are you going so early? he said	134
Plays a child in a garden fair	82

	PAGE
Pluck not the wayside-flower.	57
Plutus, God of Riches, at thy shrine	90
Ring-ting! I wish I were a Primrose	164
Saint Valentine kindles the crocus.	42
Seek up and down, both fair and brown	153
Seven years gone, and we together	288
She had nine noble brothers.	194
Slow drags this dreary season	107
Sound of feet in the lonely street.	5
Splendidly Jupiter's Planet rises over the river	96
Stream flowing swiftly, what music is thine!	37
Sweet looks!—I thought them love	68
The Abbot of Inisfalen.	149
The Boy from his bedroom-window	49
The noisy sparrows in our clematis	295
The plunging storm flies fierce against the pane	22
The roads are long and rough, with many a bend	217
These little Songs	3
These walls of green, my Emmeline	279
The shadow Death o'er Time's broad dial creeps	241
The tangling wealth by June amass'd	31
The time of Frost is the time for me!	80
The vast and solemn company of clouds.	21
The Wife sat thoughtfully turning over.	203
The wind shakes up the sleepy clouds	72
This dark-brown curl you send me, Dear	74
Tho' every dear perfection	116
Thou that hast a daughter	210
'Twas nigh the hour of evening pray'r	204
'Twas when the spinning-room was here	184
Up the airy mountain.	158
We all keep step to the marching chorus	113
Weary and wasted, nigh worn-out.	114
What can better please.	13
What is it that is gone, we fancied ours?	44

	PAGE
What knowest thou of this eternal code?	99
What saith the river to the rushes gray	20
When summer days are hot and blue	305
Where mountains round a lonely dale	206
Where these green mounds o'erlook the mingling Erne	83
Where's Lucy? where's Lucy?	166
Whither goest, brother Elf?	173
With grief and mourning I sit to spin	146
Within a budding grove	27
Ye coax the timid verdure	33
You sweet fastidious Nightingales!	111

THE END.

CHISWICK PRESS:—CHARLES WHITTINGHAM,
TOOKS COURT, CHANCERY LANE.

www.ingramcontent.com/pod-product-compliance
Lightning Source LLC
Chambersburg PA
CBHW032357230426
43672CB00007B/732